LIFE IS A PARTY

LIFE IS A PARTY

DELICIOUSLY DOABLE RECIPES TO MAKE EVERY DAY A CELEBRATION

DAVID BURTKA

With Adeena Sussman · Photographs by Amy Neunsinger · Lifestyle photographs by Danielle Levitt

GRAND CENTRAL PUBLISHING

New York Boston

Grand Central Publishing
Hachette Book Group
1290 Avenue of the Americas, New York, NY 10104
grandcentralpublishing.com
twitter.com/grandcentralpub

First Edition: April 2019

Grand Central Publishing is a division of Hachette Book Group, Inc. The Grand Central Publishing name and logo is a trademark of Hachette Book Group, Inc.

The publisher is not responsible for websites (or their content) that are not owned by the publisher.

The Hachette Speakers Bureau provides a wide range of authors for speaking events. To find out more, go to www.hachettespeakersbureau.com or call (866) 376-6591.

Print book interior design by Laura Palese Design

Library of Congress Cataloging-in-Publication Data
Names: Burtka, David, author. | Sussman, Adeena, author. | Neunsinger, Amy, photographer.
Title: Life is a party : deliciously doable recipes to make every day a celebration / David Burtka with Adeena Sussman ; photographs by Amy Neunsinger.
Description: New York : Grand Central Life and Style, 2019. | Includes index.
Identifiers: LCCN 2018044759 | ISBN 9781538729892 (hardcover) | ISBN 9781538729915 (e-book)
Subjects: LCSH: Cooking. | LCGFT: Cookbooks.
Classification: LCC TX714 .B874 2019 | DDC 641.5—dc23
LC record available at https://lccn.loc.gov/2018044759

ISBNs: 978-1-5387-2989-2 (hardcover); 978-1-5387-2991-5 (e-book)

Printed in the United States of America

WOR

10 9 8 7 6 5 4 3 2 1

**FOR HARPER,
GIDEON, AND NEIL,**
the best sous-chefs of all time.

CONTENTS

INTRODUCTION

Welcome to my party!
I'm so excited you showed up.

IN A LIFE FULL OF OBLIGATIONS and things we *have* to do, *choosing* to create special gatherings that bring our loved ones together at the table is more important than ever. Think about the best parties you've ever been to: If you're anything like me, they've been at home (yours or someone else's), with great food and drink, amazing people, and—more than anything—fun! Because if it's not a good time, what's the point, right?

Those parties may have *seemed* effortless, but we all know they take work to pull off in style. That's where I come in! I'm so excited to share everything I've learned from a lifetime of entertaining. From the big flourishes to those tiny touches that take a party from good to great, I've collected it all right here. I want you to think of me as your personal party planner, filled with exciting, doable ideas that will make your party even more of a celebration.

I've always been a big believer in the power of parties. Parties have this magical, transformative ability to create a wonderful feeling of connectedness and happiness—it's undeniable! I mean, isn't it just the best when you arrive at a party and find yourself surrounded by familiar and new faces, lots of thoughtfully prepared food, great drinks, and the perfect music? It's like being infused with joy! I think we all need to go to and throw more parties, because we all need more of this wonderfully positive feeling in our lives on the regular. Life is too short *not* to party.

I have a large family filled with cooks and people who take food seriously, so I got the taste for catering and hosting very early in life. Every weekend, my family and a select assortment of friends would get together to eat and drink, whether it was for a birthday, a christening, or just to be together. From the time I was seven years old, I'd help my parents get ready for their parties—the party prep would start midday on Saturday and go well into the night.

My mother, who has had a huge influence on how I approach cooking and entertaining, always had a massive list of chores for me to do, and of course the ones that kept me in the kitchen were my favorites. She taught me how to make a killer crudités platter, showed me how to make stripes in cucumber skin by using a vegetable peeler and the best way to trim cauliflower and broccoli into perfect bite-size florets, and explained why you *always* need to wrap bell pepper slices in paper towels (otherwise, they get slimy). Sometimes the whole family would gather in the kitchen for hours, hand-rolling mini meatballs, enough for a party—and the rest to freeze for the remainder of the year. I learned early on that when you bring friends and family together for an event you designed with them in mind, people immediately feel special. They open up, the conversation flows, they laugh a little more—everyone seems just a little bit happier. Who doesn't want a little more of that in their lives?

After graduating from culinary school and working with some top-notch chefs, I started my own catering company and threw parties for the likes of Christina Hendricks, Katy Perry, and Elon Musk. And while the Hollywood elite may have had high standards and demands, I loved it. I thrived!

I not only create focused and delicious dishes, but also bring a party to the next level with stunning tablescapes, elaborate decorations, perfect playlists—whatever it takes to make an event what it deserves to be: memorable and fabulous.

*I loved the holidays even at a young age. Here I am
dyeing Easter eggs (with a bad haircut).*

That's why I wanted to write this book: to share what I've learned. I want everyone in the world to stop waiting for the *right* reason to throw a party, and just…throw a party! Create your *own* occasion, because every single day is worth celebrating. It can be as simple as a hunker-down-at-home-during-a-snowstorm party, a movie night for two—or a total blowout cocktail party with a bartender, bubbles, and confetti.

Over the fifteen years my husband, Neil, and I have been together, we've thrown literally thousands—okay, probably hundreds—of parties of every kind, from brunches and picnic lunches to all-out black-tie bashes. We don't hold back!

So how do I do it? Well, a successful party is much more about the sum of its parts than it is about just one detail. I've been acting since I was a child, and I have realized that while an actor's performance is important, it is lost if the scene itself isn't fully realized. Sure, I can assume a new identity with a uniquely delivered line, or captivate a crowd with a rousing musical number, but that tells only half the story—the rest is told through ambience, wardrobe, lighting, music, props, and, of course, the set. A dynamite dinner party is no different.

You can serve delicious, bite-size morsels and mix the perfect cocktail, but if you haven't set up your room to allow for space and flow, how will your guests mingle? If the music is too loud, how will they talk? If the time you choose to throw your party doesn't make sense—I'm thinking a kid's birthday party too late in the evening during the witching hour!—people might feel uncomfortable and not have a good time. Just as with acting, if you're prepared and have approached the party with thoughtfulness and care, if you've put the right elements in place and invested in making the occasion special, you can open that front door feeling confident that a great gathering is under way.

Dinner is a meal, but a dinner *party* has the opportunity to be an *event*.

I DECIDED TO ORGANIZE THIS BOOK by season, with quintessential holiday-specific parties as well as "anytime" gatherings, because that's how we organize our lives—from big event to small, based on our schedules and also what produce is the freshest. My hope is that the ideas, advice, photos, and encouragement on the following pages will fill your inspiration tank until it's brimming with ideas, and also give you practical strategies for making any party seem as effortless as it is exciting. And let's be real—no one wants to see a stressed-out host, either before or during a party. A party should be fun for everyone…including *you*!

I'll also share recipes that I've created for many a memorable occasion. Some are family classics that I've given a twist, while others are from my years of cooking, both pre- and post-kids, for clients, teachers, parents, and friends. After Neil and I had our kids, Harper and Gideon, we didn't stop entertaining. We simply reconfigured how we entertain. Sometimes that means parties that the whole family can enjoy (and you'll find several of them throughout *Life Is a Party*), and sometimes it means adults-only parties (and *yes*, you really do need to be explicit on those invites!).

Oh, and speaking of invites—one of the most exciting things I've learned is that once you send the invitation, congratulations—you've already won! The good-time gathering gears are officially set in motion. People tend to love a party, and arrive primed to celebrate, dine, dance, and savor the few hours of bliss you're offering them. They don't care so much about the perfect placement of the chives or whether the napkin is folded with exact precision; they've come to connect, to indulge, to enjoy—and you've made that possible. It's a good feeling.

So enjoy the hard-earned wisdom and instruction on the pages of this book. You can follow every suggestion step-by-step, from start to finish, or you can pick and choose different elements and ideas to incorporate into any celebration. It's entirely up to you. But if I've learned anything, it's this: If you get stressed in the process of planning, don't worry. Just take a deep breath (and perhaps a sip of wine!) and remember that it's *allllll* good. Who you've brought to the table counts as much as what you put on it.

Welcome to the party! Now turn the page, and let's have some fun!

Dinner is a
meal,
but a dinner
party has the
opportunity
to be an
event.

BURTKA'S
RULES

THE REAL DEAL

Try to avoid plastic—real plates, flatware, and napkins make people feel more special…and are better for the environment (if it's a kid-centric party, then this rule can be bent—or opt for those snazzy and eco-friendly bamboo plates and utensils). If you are using real linens, make sure you iron your napkins and tablecloths. I once helped Sharon Stone with a party in Hollywood. She insisted on serving KFC on fancy china. It looked great, and no one had any idea. If you're feeling overwhelmed by the thought of washing dishes, ask your guests to chip in, consider hiring some help (even a teen who wants to earn a few bucks!), or rent dishes and glassware, which can be returned dirty (hallelujah!).

THINK AHEAD

The more you can plan and do ahead of time, the more you'll be able to enjoy your own party. Make a list of everything from shopping to an hour-by-hour party-prep countdown. Set up your table the night before: Lay the tablecloth and arrange the empty serving pieces exactly where you want them to go. Use sticky notes to designate which dishes will be going in which vessels. I even like to pick out what I'm wearing the night before! The less you have to do the day of, the better.

MOOD PREP

Listen to playlists while prepping for your party; this gets you in a festive mood and also allows you to make any last-minute additions to your music! Leave yourself Post-its around the kitchen, if that helps. The night before, while you are setting the table, do a dry run. Make sure the lighting is right. And the more candles, the better. I love a moody room—plus, everyone looks ten years younger!

SHOP OUT

If you're feeling overwhelmed (don't worry, I do, too!), take advantage of the best shops in your neighborhood and treat them like caterers to fill any hole in your menu and impress your guests. And don't be afraid to take advantage of technology to make your life easier; order from online stores like Goldbelly for specialty or hard-to-find foods and Amazon, Instacart, or FreshDirect for pantry staples. This frees you up to hit the best market in town for star ingredients like produce, herbs, or that special cut of meat.

ICE, ICE, BABY

Never, ever run out of ice! It's essential for mixing drinks, keeping beverages cool—even for many cooking tasks. Have bags of ice delivered the day of the party. Or, if you have the room, start filling, freezing, and emptying ice into zip-top bags a few days before the party. If you don't have room for multiple bags of ice in your freezer, keep them in the bathtub, or even the washing machine. A good rule is one pound (or about 2½ cups) of ice per guest.

INSTANT FEED

You should always offer your guest a drink upon arrival; people feel more comfortable with something in their hand. Also, set some food out right when people get there—we're not the kind of household where people stare longingly at an empty table, waiting for the first tastes to come out of the kitchen. However, make those first bites small: nuts, olives, and bar mix are all perfect. If you are serving appetizers, make sure they are one-bite snacks. People are coming to eat as the main event, so give them what they came for!

The kids love **helping** me in the kitchen, especially when making **dessert**.

DON'T BE NUTTY

Make sure to ask your guests if they have any food allergies or if there are any foods they strongly dislike. It's always nice to make people who can't eat everything feel special; it's hard enough having a nut allergy and never being able to eat peanut butter.

MORE IS MORE

It's better to have extra food than to run out—there's nothing worse than being at a party and seeing the sad bottom of empty platters and drink pitchers. So make a little extra! Not only will your guests feel spoiled, but it will give you piece of mind before, during, and after your party. You can always send friends home with leftovers in plastic containers or Chinese takeout boxes. Also, make sure your bathroom is stocked with hand towels and toilet paper, and light a nice seasonal candle.

IT DOESN'T HAVE TO END

Have post-dinner entertainment in the form of a piano-playing friend, a spirited game, or a movie screening—something to shift the mood. The party doesn't have to stop just because the dessert has been served.

ADULTS LIKE GOODIE BAGS, TOO!

I always like to send people home with something. It doesn't have to be overly elaborate or complicated, just a token that conveys, "Thank you for coming!": a signature holiday cookie wrapped in cellophane, or a bag of granola in a paper bag hand-inscribed with the recipe. You could also go with a little craft project you (or you and your kids) have made, either before or at the party itself.

DON'T BE AFRAID TO COHOST

Pooling resources with a trusted party partner has a ton of advantages. Not only can you divide and conquer—which saves you time and money—but it brings new ideas, recipes, and energy to the process.

GET THE KIDS INVOLVED

Kids can get a little stir-crazy in the days and hours before a big gathering, so have them do things like polishing silver, folding napkins, and picking out their party outfits so they feel engaged in the process. My mom made my sister and me her personal assistants when getting ready for her cocktail parties. I might have complained in the past, but I am thankful for it now. She not only nurtured a strong work ethic in me, but now I have all these great skills for throwing a party.

PICKING THE RIGHT GROUP

Spend a few minutes in advance thinking about what people have in common, both on the surface and beyond the expected. Who grew up in the Midwest? Who is really passionate about a hobby? A scientist with an art dealer? Yes—the more eclectic and interesting, the better! My favorite number for an intimate dinner is eight. It allows for a few single conversations, or the whole group can get in on one juicy topic.

BECOME A SEATING JEDI MASTER

There is an art to seating people, and it's not always the obvious choice that yields the most sparkling dinner-party conversations. I always feel that sitting next to someone I know nothing about is fun. My friend Lizzie Tisch (the consummate party hostess) says, "If they sleep together, don't sit them together." Sit the big personalities in the middle of the table; they will help the flow of the conversation. As you set the table, use place cards for the guest seating chart. I like to put the name on the front *and* the back, in case people don't know each other.

UNPLUG

Trust me, you can live without your cell phone for an hour or so. We have a big rule at our house: no electronics at the table. There is also a fun game you can play: Have all your guests stack their cell phones in the middle of the table, and the first person to grab for their device has to do all the dishes—or pay the check the next time you go out to dinner.

DIG-IN BRUNCH

DIY Soda Bar 9

Greek Frittata with Ramps and Chickpeas 10

Fava Bean and English Pea Salad with
Lemon Vinaigrette and Pecorino 13

Rhubarb-Ginger Crumb Muffins 14

Cumin-Roasted Carrots with Lemony Yogurt
and Cilantro 17

Roast Chicken 18

Spring has sprung! Reconnect with your roots by gathering family and friends, young and old, for a late-morning or early afternoon outdoor gardening party, complete with a fresh and exciting buffet of spring explosion that is sure to awaken your appetite. Since it's still early spring, the sun shouldn't be too intense and there won't be a lot of bugs to keep at bay, perfect for setting up the food and enjoying it outside. I purposefully selected dishes that can be set out and left at room temperature; nothing needs to be served hot, and the only item you need to remember to keep cold is the drinks (and a cute ice bucket gets that job done!).

WHAT GUESTS CAN BRING

Ask your guests to bring one or some of the following: cut or potted spring flowers, birdseed, pinecones for making bird feeders, or seed packs of local wildflowers for planting a butterfly garden.

GET GUESTS INVOLVED

If young ones are coming, keep them occupied by making sure there are plenty of crafts and activities ready to begin. Grown-up guests can help set up the soda bar, organize all the gardening tools, dress the salad, and get the pinecone bird-feeder craft organized.

WHAT TO WEAR

If you plan to get dirty, put on overalls, old jeans, boots, and gloves for digging (and have a few spare pieces ready for friends who decide to dig in at the spur of the moment). If messy work and you don't mix, then this is the perfect opportunity to break out your favorite flowery sundress or a seersucker jacket.

THE TABLE

Make your table look like a garden! Use sanded tree stumps or thick segments of logs as trivets or risers. You can also use bricks and gardening crates as stands for elevating food.

THE FLOWERS

Potted spring plants like paper lilies, tulips, daffodils, and hyacinths are pretty, as are spring greens like ferns, potted fresh herbs, and wheatgrass. Feel free to make arrangements in old watering cans.

PARTY BASICS

Get out your SodaStream or other home seltzer maker and have a fresh canister of CO_2 ready for action to make Italian sodas (see DIY Soda Bar, page 9)! Decant your flavored syrups into spouted bottles for easy pouring. Use gardening shovels as servingware. Make a garden garland out of twine, clothespins, and seed packs. Bring the outside in! Hang cut branches of flowering trees (forsythia, cherry blossoms, pussy willow, etc.) from chandeliers, and arrange them like art on the walls of your house using thumbtacks or double-sided foam tape.

PARTY UPGRADES

Make a "cloud" out of cotton and use twine to hang small crystals from the cloud—when the sun shines through the crystals, rainbows materialize! Cover food platters and serving dishes with a lush bed of herbs before setting food on top. Use medium-size terra-cotta pots for storing utensils, and smaller pots for serving crudités—place dip, guacamole, or hummus in the bottom of the pots! Make a dessert bar with spring-themed candies (gummy worms, sour flowers, etc.), using small terra-cotta pots for serving.

OVER-THE-TOP IDEAS

Buy a roll of grass sod and use it as a table runner. Get a wheelbarrow and fill it with ice and bottles of Champagne or vodka for an adults-only spritzer station. Roll linen napkins and fasten them with wire, herbs, and spring flowers. Order live ladybugs online (yes, this is a thing!) for a bug release— butterflies are a great idea, too. Grow moss on a piece of stretched canvas, then hang it in the garden or in the kitchen. Instead of serving plain ice, freeze an edible flower in each cube. Make flower crowns and wreaths for guests—or set up a craft station where they can make them themselves!

PLAN AHEAD

Set up the party and food outside, but in case of rain (or the freak spring snowstorm!), make sure you have a dedicated indoor spot (yes, that means cleared, cleaned, and ready for action) to bring all the food, drinks, and dishes, just in case.

- *Three Days Before:* Make and freeze the muffins; make the soda syrups.
- *Two Days Before:* Prep the fava beans and peas; make the dressing and lemony yogurt sauce.
- *One Day Before:* Chop herbs; prep the frittata.

KEEP THE PARTY GOING

Watch *The Secret Garden* or set up a croquet course. Lay out a variety of flowers and have guests guess which variety is which; whoever identifies the highest number takes home the flowers in a vase. Provide roll-out sugar cookie dough and have the kids (and adults) decorate their cookies with floral motifs.

Make simple terrariums. Provide mason jars or terrarium glass containers and a variety of sands, succulent plants, stones, and miniature sprites, fairies, and toadstools so people can make their own terrariums.

Set up a rock-painting station for the kids. Encourage them to create their own theme that they can then incorporate into their own gardens.

HOST CRAFT PROJECT

MINIATURE PAINTED POTS

Create a DIY flowerpot–painting station with terra-cotta pots, brushes, and paints (supply smocks or toss-away thrift-shop button-down shirts for guests).

THE DRINKS

Use a giant galvanized steel gardening bucket or a trough for chilling beverages. Stock up on multiple bottles of soda water, or a home seltzer maker for the DIY Soda Bar (page 9), with syrups stored in plastic squeeze bottles.

ACTIVITIES

Weed, dig, and sow seeds in the garden; paint terra-cotta pots and fill them with dirt and plant seeds (these are a take-home gift that will remind your guests of your party for weeks—and potentially months—to come).

GIFTS FOR GUESTS

Packages of seeds and pinecones; gardening starter kits (pair of gloves, shovel, watering can); fresh-cut flowers.

PARTY PROJECT

NUT AND SEED PINECONE BIRD FEEDER

Tie string around the top of a pinecone, then coat it with nut butter or honey, followed by seeds and nuts (think sunflower seeds, poppy seeds, chopped peanuts, and sesame seeds). Don't be afraid to push the seeds into the center! Hang the pinecone outside and watch the birds go to town.

PLAYLIST

Stream all the extended playlists on Spotify at spoti.fi/davidburtka.

"The Garden/All in the Afternoon," from *Alice in Wonderland*, Disney Studio Chorus

"Garden Song," John Denver

"Deep Purple," Artie Shaw and Helen Forrest

"Gardening at Night," REM

"Garden Party," Rick Nelson

"The Magic Garden," The 5th Dimension

"In the Garden of Mystic Lovers," Francis Dunnery

"Leaves That Are Green," Simon and Garfunkel

"Mr. Farmer," The Seeds

"Little April Shower," from the *Bambi* sound track

"Octopus's Garden," The Beatles

"Stormy Weather," Etta James

"I Can See Clearly Now," Johnny Nash

Packaged in **flip-top glass bottles**, these syrups also make **great host gifts**.

DIY SODA BAR

SIMPLE SYRUP

4 cups sugar

4 cups water

MANGO-MANDARIN MINT SODA

2 cups cubed mango (about 2 small or 1 large)

3 clementines or seedless mandarins, peeled

Leaves from 4 sprigs mint

CELERY-BASIL SODA

2 cups chopped celery (about 3 large stalks)

Leaves from 1 (2-ounce) bunch basil (about 2 cups)

STRAWBERRY-RHUBARB SODA

2 cups chopped rhubarb (about 2 large stalks)

2 cups chopped hulled strawberries (about 14 large)

6 liters soda water, for serving

Ice

1. Make the simple syrup: In a large saucepan, heat the sugar and water over medium heat, stirring frequently, until the sugar has completely dissolved. Set aside to cool (you should have about 6 cups simple syrup).

2. To make mango-mandarin mint soda: In a blender, combine 2 cups of the cooled simple syrup, the mango, clementines, and mint and blend until smooth, then strain through a fine-mesh sieve (you should have about 3 cups mango-mandarin syrup).

To make celery-basil soda: In a blender, combine 2 cups of the cooled simple syrup, the celery, and the basil and blend until smooth, then strain through a fine-mesh sieve (you should have about 3 cups celery-basil syrup).

To make strawberry-rhubarb soda: In a small saucepan, combine 2 cups of the cooled simple syrup and the chopped rhubarb and bring to a boil over high heat. Cook until the rhubarb softens and can easily be pierced with a fork, about 5 minutes. Set aside to cool slightly, then transfer to a blender, add the strawberries, and blend until smooth. Strain through a fine-mesh sieve (you should have about 3 cups strawberry-rhubarb syrup).

3. Pour the syrups into flip-top or squeeze bottles and refrigerate until cold (the syrups can be refrigerated for up to 15 days). When it's time for the party, arrange a soda bar with the syrups, soda water, ice, and tall glasses. To make each soda, fill a glass with ice, then add enough soda water to come within 1 inch of the rim (about 6 ounces or ¾ cup). Squeeze about ¼ cup of the soda syrup into the glass, adding more or less to taste, stir, and enjoy!

MAKES
3 CUPS
of each flavor
soda syrup

—

about
12 servings
of each flavor

PREP TIME
15 minutes

COOK TIME
15 minutes

TOTAL TIME
30 minutes

EASY

Ditch the canned soda and serve this simple homemade version instead!

GREEK FRITTATA

WITH RAMPS AND CHICKPEAS

1 large bunch ramps (about 4 ounces), cleaned, bulbs and greens separated

3 tablespoons olive oil

Kosher salt and freshly ground black pepper

1 (15.5-ounce) can chickpeas, drained and rinsed

4 cups packed baby spinach (5 ounces)

¼ cup pitted Kalamata olives (about 12)

½ cup oil-packed sun-dried tomatoes (about 10), with a hefty splash of the oil they're packed in reserved

½ teaspoon dried oregano

12 large eggs

6 ounces Greek feta cheese in brine, drained and crumbled into large pieces

1. Preheat the oven to 350°F.

2. In an 8-inch square baking dish, toss the ramp bulbs with 1 tablespoon of the olive oil and a pinch each of salt and pepper. Bake, stirring midway through, until tender and lightly browned, about 20 minutes. Remove from the oven and let the ramp bulbs cool slightly, then transfer to a cutting board and coarsely chop. Add the chickpeas to the same baking dish you used to cook the ramp bulbs. Set aside.

3. Slice the ramp greens into 1-inch pieces. In a large skillet, heat the remaining 2 tablespoons olive oil over medium heat. Add the ramp greens and the spinach to the pan and season with a pinch each of salt and pepper (you may need to cook the greens in batches). Cook, stirring occasionally, until the ramp greens and spinach are just wilted, about 5 minutes, then transfer to a bowl.

4. Top the chickpeas in the baking dish evenly with the wilted greens, chopped ramp bulbs, olives, sun-dried tomatoes with a splash of their oil, and oregano.

5. In a medium bowl, whisk the eggs with a large pinch each of salt and pepper until well combined. Evenly pour the eggs over the ramps in the baking dish and sprinkle with the feta.

6. Bake until the top is lightly browned in spots and the frittata is mostly set but still jiggles a bit in the center when you lightly shake the baking dish, about 50 minutes, rotating the baking dish halfway through cooking. Set aside to cool for at least 20 minutes (the frittata will continue to cook as it cools).

7. Cut the frittata into 8 large or 12 smaller pieces and serve warm or at room temperature.

SERVES 8 TO 12

PREP TIME
15 minutes

ACTIVE TIME
20 minutes

TOTAL TIME
1 hour 30 minutes
(includes baking and cooling time.)

EASY

Vegetarians go crazy for this protein-packed dish, which can be served hot or at room temperature.

FAVA BEAN AND ENGLISH PEA SALAD

WITH LEMON VINAIGRETTE AND PECORINO

Favas are a labor of love, a lot of love—and worth it! Shelling the beans is a great job for kids—they love the challenge, and it keeps little hands busy while you get other tasks done.

Kosher salt and freshly ground black pepper

3 pounds fava beans, shelled

1½ cups English peas, shelled

Juice of ½ lemon (about 2 tablespoons)

1 teaspoon Dijon mustard

¼ cup extra-virgin olive oil

4 cups arugula leaves, pea shoots, or a mix

Leaves from 1 bunch mint (about 2 cups)

3 ounces Pecorino Romano, shaved (about ⅔ cup)

½ cup shelled roasted pistachios, coarsely chopped

1. Bring a medium pot of heavily salted water to a boil (the water should taste like the sea). Add the fava beans and cook until they rise to the surface, 30 seconds to 1 minute. Use a slotted spoon to transfer the beans to a medium bowl and let cool. Add the peas to the boiling water and cook until they turn bright green, about 1 minute. Drain the peas in a colander and set aside to cool.

2. Once the favas have cooled, gently squeeze the beans out of their skins; they should be bright green and tender. Discard the skins and set the peeled favas aside in a large bowl.

3. In a medium bowl, whisk together the lemon juice, mustard, ½ teaspoon salt, and ¼ teaspoon pepper. While whisking, slowly drizzle in the olive oil and whisk until the dressing is emulsified and creamy.

4. Add the arugula leaves and/or pea shoots, mint, peas, Pecorino, and half the pistachios to the bowl with the favas and toss to combine. Transfer the salad to a large platter and scatter the remaining pistachios on top. Wait to dress the salad until right before serving so the greens don't get soggy.

SERVES 6 TO 8

PREP TIME
30 minutes

ACTIVE TIME
15 minutes

TOTAL TIME
50 minutes

EASY

CRUMB MUFFINS

My kids are such huge fans of these—an entire batch can literally be gone in a day! When we photographed these for the book and had to set the most beautiful muffins aside for the camera, the kids were so disappointed. The earthiness of the rhubarb, the spiciness of the ginger, and the delicious topping...they all complement each other so well.

FOR THE CRUMB TOPPING

⅓ cup all-purpose flour

¼ cup old-fashioned rolled oats

⅓ cup lightly packed light brown sugar

½ cup finely chopped crystallized ginger

Kosher salt

5 tablespoons unsalted butter, at room temperature

FOR THE MUFFINS

2 cups all-purpose flour

2 teaspoons ground ginger

2 teaspoons baking powder

½ teaspoon baking soda

½ teaspoon fine salt

½ cup (1 stick) unsalted butter, at room temperature

1 cup lightly packed light brown sugar

1 tablespoon finely grated orange zest

2 large eggs

½ cup buttermilk

2 teaspoons vanilla extract

1½ cups diced rhubarb (2 to 3 stalks)

1. Preheat the oven to 375°F. Line a 12-cup muffin pan with paper liners.

2. Make the crumb topping: In a medium bowl, whisk together the flour, oats, brown sugar, ginger, and a pinch of salt. Add the butter and use your fingers to work it into the flour mixture until a crumbly, streusel-like texture forms. Set aside.

3. Make the batter: In a medium bowl, whisk together the flour, ginger, baking powder, baking soda, and salt.

4. In the bowl of a stand mixer fitted with the paddle attachment, beat the butter, brown sugar, and orange zest on medium speed until pale and fluffy, about 4 minutes. Reduce the speed to medium-low and add the eggs one at a time, scraping down the sides of the bowl with a rubber spatula after each addition. Mix until incorporated (the mixture will look broken or curdled, and that's okay).

5. Reduce the mixer speed to low. Add half the flour mixture, then the buttermilk and vanilla, followed by the rest of the flour mixture, scraping down the sides of the bowl as needed. Turn off the mixer and fold in the rhubarb with a spatula.

6. Divide the batter among the prepared muffin cups (use about ⅓ cup batter for each muffin). Top with a heaping tablespoon of the crumb topping, pressing it lightly to ensure the mixture adheres. Bake until a toothpick inserted into the center of a muffin comes out clean, 25 to 30 minutes. Let the muffins cool in the pan on a wire rack for 30 minutes before serving. They can be stored in a single layer in an airtight container for up to 5 days at room temperature or 10 days refrigerated.

MAKES 12 MUFFINS

PREP TIME
20 minutes

ACTIVE TIME
20 minutes

TOTAL TIME
1 hour 40 minutes

EASY

Make a double batch— these babies go fast! Look for rainbow carrots, and if they're more than an inch in diameter, slice them in half lengthwise.

CUMIN-ROASTED CARROTS

WITH LEMONY YOGURT AND CILANTRO

1 tablespoon cumin seeds

1 bunch multicolored carrots (about 1 pound), trimmed

2 tablespoons olive oil

Kosher salt

½ cup low-fat Greek yogurt

Grated zest and juice of 1 medium lemon

¼ cup lightly packed fresh cilantro leaves, for garnish

SPECIAL EQUIPMENT
spice grinder

> While I love toasting and grinding my own spices, feel free to substitute in the same amount of dried spices whenever you need to.

1. Preheat the oven to 425°F. Set a baking sheet in the oven to heat up while you prep the ingredients.

2. In a small dry skillet, toast the cumin seeds over medium heat, stirring occasionally, until fragrant, 2 to 3 minutes. Transfer the cumin to a plate to cool completely, then use a spice grinder to grind the seeds into a fine powder.

3. In a medium bowl, toss together the carrots, olive oil, ground cumin, and a large pinch of salt. Carefully remove the hot baking sheet from the oven and add the carrots, shaking the pan to make sure the carrots are in a single layer but not touching one another. Roast until the carrots are tender and deeply charred in spots, 20 to 25 minutes, shaking the pan halfway through.

4. Meanwhile, in a small bowl, whisk together the yogurt, lemon zest, lemon juice, and a large pinch of salt. Spread the yogurt sauce in the center of a large serving platter, top with the carrots, and sprinkle with the cilantro. Serve immediately.

SERVES 4 TO 6

PREP TIME
10 minutes

ACTIVE TIME
15 minutes

TOTAL TIME
50 minutes

EASY

ROAST CHICKEN

2 whole chickens (about 4 pounds each), patted dry

Sea salt and freshly ground black pepper

Big handful of fresh herbs, such as thyme, oregano, and rosemary

2 lemons, halved

3 leeks or purple spring onions, quartered lengthwise and rinsed well

2 red onions, each cut into 8 wedges

2 pounds small Yukon Gold potatoes, scrubbed and halved

½ cup dry white wine (optional)

MAKE A
PAN SAUCE

To make things extra fancy, make a pan sauce: Once the chickens and vegetables are removed from the roasting pan, set the pan on the stovetop over medium-high heat. Cook until the drippings start to bubble, then pour in the white wine and use a wooden spoon to scrape up the brown bits from the bottom of the pan. Continue stirring until the pan is completely deglazed (all the brown bits are unstuck), the wine has burned off its alcohol, and the mixture resembles a sauce, 3 to 4 minutes. You can also whisk in 1 tablespoon of all-purpose or Wondra flour to make a quick gravy. Pour the pan sauce over the carved chicken and serve at once.

1. Preheat the oven to 425°F.

2. Season the chickens inside and out with a healthy amount of salt and pepper. Stuff the chickens with the fresh herbs and lemon halves, then truss the legs with kitchen twine. (See page 21 for instructions.) Put the leeks, onions, and potatoes into a large roasting pan. Nestle the chickens over the vegetables, breast-side up, making sure the chickens do not touch each other.

3. Roast, uncovered, until the chickens are golden brown and cooked through, about 1 hour 30 minutes. When the chickens are fully cooked, the juices will run clear when the thigh meat is poked with a sharp knife and the legs will move easily when wiggled; an instant-read thermometer inserted into the thickest part of the breast should read 165°F. Remove the roasting pan from the oven and let the chickens stand for 15 minutes before carving. Serve the chicken family-style on a large platter, together with the vegetables.

(See page 21 for instructions.)

SERVES 8

PREP TIME
15 minutes

ACTIVE TIME
15 minutes

TOTAL TIME
2 hours

EASY

I always make roast chicken in pairs: The second one provides protein for a salad bar or a delicious soup (and a million other possibilities).

1

With the chicken breast-side up, tuck the wings under the body of the bird and wrap kitchen twine around the neck.

2

Wrap the twine around the drumsticks and under their joints.

3

Cross over the drumstick joints.

4

Tighten to bring the drumsticks together and plump up the breasts.

5

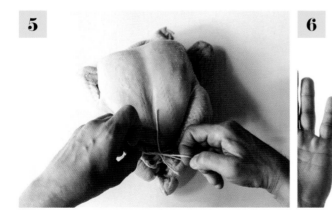

Secure the twine with a knot.

6

Voilà!

HOW
TO
TIE A
CHICKEN

THANK-YOU DINNER

Cucumber-Herb Cocktail 26

Scallops with Peas and Green Oil 29

Braised Beef Brisket with Carrots and Tomatoes 30

Mixed Greens with Fennel and Pink Grapefruit 33

Grilled Baby Artichokes with Zesty Vinaigrette 34

Flourless Chocolate Cake with Almond
Whipped Cream 36

Gratitude gives you latitude! Take the chance to pamper those in your life who've gone above and beyond on your behalf with an evening of tributes and amazing food. Whether it's a boss or coworker, a family member, a beloved teacher, or a friend who always goes the extra mile, you'll feel as good as they do when you spoil them from start to finish. This is also a great menu for graduations, promotions, honors, Mother's Day, and more. Choose a spring weekend as the weather starts to get nicer and invite guests to your home; if it's warm enough, make it the first outdoor dinner of the season.

PARTY BASICS

Food is planned out, flowers on the table, elevated level of décor, a handwritten thank-you note for the guest of honor.

PARTY UPGRADES

Boutonnieres, corsages, prepared speeches, flower crowns.

OVER-THE-TOP IDEAS

Pre-order customized cookies and candy online (just make sure to leave enough time for delivery). Put together a slide show honoring your guest(s). Several weeks before, make an iBook of all your favorite photographs of you and your guest(s).

WHAT GUESTS CAN BRING
Themselves—this night is about them!

GET GUESTS INVOLVED
Put your spouse or significant other to work, hire help, or host the party with a friend—anything to make sure your guests don't have to help. Order them to take a load off and have a relaxing night that's all about them.

WHAT TO WEAR
Dress up so your guests feel special—but not so over the top that they feel underdressed.

THE TABLE
A white tablecloth, nice dishes, flatware, and cloth napkins. Spend a little time online learning how to execute that extra-special napkin fold. Seat the guest(s) of honor at the head of the table.

THE FLOWERS
Peonies, tulips, ranunculus, poppies, dahlias. Make special corsages, boutonnieres, and flower crowns to make them feel extra honored.

THE DRINKS
Cucumber-Herb or French 75 cocktails, nice bottles of wine—dry Riesling or Chardonnay for the scallops, Barolo for the brisket.

HOST CRAFT PROJECT
Make hand-decorated thank-you cards; frame photographs of the honoree with you and other mutual friends.

PLAN AHEAD
- *Three Days Before:* Make the green oil and zesty vinaigrette.
- *Two Days Before:* Prepare the simple syrup for the cocktail. Prepare the mixed green salad. Cut the fennel and grapefruits; peel the carrots and potatoes and keep them submerged in water.
- *One Day Before:* Prepare the brisket; make the chocolate cake. Make the flower crown, corsages, and boutonnieres.

ACTIVITIES
Get together with a friend and orchestrate an at-home version of *This Is Your Life*, where you highlight the guest of honor's major accomplishments. Create a Mad Lib with clues about your guests. Set up a video recording booth where people can record stories about and thank-yous for the guest(s) of honor.

PARTY PROJECT
Blow up a big picture at the local copy store and have everyone sign it. Create a hand-decorated gratitude book for guests to fill in with personal sentiments and salutations.

GIFTS FOR GUESTS
Do a little detective work about the guest of honor's favorite music, then send everyone home with a flash-drive playlist.

KEEP THE PARTY GOING
Set up a faux podium and conduct a Comedy Central–style roast, complete with musical performances.

PLAYLIST

"It Might as Well Be Spring,"
Sarah Vaughan

"Pocketful of Sunshine,"
Natasha Bedingfield

"April in Paris," Ella Fitzgerald
and Louis Armstrong

"Southland in the Springtime,"
Indigo Girls

"Blossom/Meadow,"
George Winston

"Spring Is Here," Nina Simone

"Some Other Spring,"
Billie Holiday

"April Come She Will,"
Simon and Garfunkel

"You Must Believe in Spring,"
Bill Evans

"Spring Vacation,"
The Beach Boys

**"You Are the Sunshine of My
Life,"** Stevie Wonder

"Walking on Sunshine,"
Katrina and the Waves

CUCUMBER-HERB COCKTAIL

1 Persian cucumber, chopped

10 fresh basil leaves

Ice

3 ounces vodka

3 tablespoons fresh lemon juice (about 1 lemon)

2 tablespoons simple syrup (see page 9)

1 ounce green Chartreuse liqueur

1 English cucumber, shaved into long ribbons (1 ribbon per serving)

2 edible flowers, such as pansies or violets (optional)

1. Put the chopped Persian cucumber and the basil leaves in a cocktail shaker and muddle until well smashed and fragrant. Add a few ice cubes, then pour in the vodka, lemon juice, simple syrup, and Chartreuse.

2. Place the top on the shaker and shake like the dickens, about 20 seconds. Pour through a fine-mesh strainer into two rocks glasses filled with ice. Garnish each with a cucumber ribbon and an edible flower.

MAKES 2 DRINKS

PREP TIME
5 minutes

ACTIVE TIME
5 minutes

TOTAL TIME
10 minutes

EASY

CUCUMBER-HERB MOCKTAIL

Omit the Chartreuse and replace the vodka with ½ cup of a nonalcoholic spirit, such as Seedlip.

SCALLOPS

WITH PEAS AND GREEN OIL

This recipe will make more green oil than you'll need, but it keeps for months in the refrigerator and can be used in other applications—on salads or grilled vegetables, even drizzled on toast.

12 large sea scallops (about 1 pound)

¼ cup pine nuts

1 large bunch flat-leaf parsley

1 cup olive oil

Kosher salt and freshly ground black pepper

1 pound English peas, shelled (about 2 cups)

¼ cup water

4 tablespoons clarified butter or ghee

Juice of 1 small Meyer lemon (about 2 tablespoons)

1 tablespoon thinly sliced fresh chives

SPECIAL EQUIPMENT
fish spatula

1. Preheat the oven to 350°F.

2. Place the scallops on a plate lined with paper towels. Refrigerate, uncovered, while you prep the rest of the ingredients. (This helps create a nice crust when you sear them.)

3. Spread the pine nuts over a small baking sheet and toast in the oven until very lightly browned and fragrant, 6 to 8 minutes. Check the nuts frequently. Transfer to a plate and set aside.

4. In a blender, combine the parsley (stems included), olive oil, and a pinch of salt and blend until completely smooth. Strain the mixture through a fine-mesh sieve into a bowl, pressing on the solids with a rubber spatula to extract all the juice. Discard the pulp and set the green oil aside.

5. Bring a medium saucepan of heavily salted water to a boil (the water should taste like the sea). Add the peas and cook until they are bright green and crisp-tender, about 1 minute. Drain and let cool slightly. Place the peas in the blender with 1 tablespoon of the green oil, the water, and a large pinch each of salt and pepper. Blend until the peas make a chunky puree, then taste and season with additional salt and pepper.

6. Remove the scallops from the refrigerator and pat dry once more. Season liberally with salt and pepper. Heat a large skillet over high heat. Add 2 tablespoons of the clarified butter and swirl the pan to coat, then immediately add 6 of the scallops and cook, untouched, for 1½ minutes. Use a fish spatula or thin metal spatula to flip the scallops and cook for 1½ minutes on the second side, using a large metal spoon and tilting the pan as needed to baste the scallops with the butter. Transfer the cooked scallops to a large plate and carefully wipe out the pan. Repeat, using the remaining 2 tablespoons clarified butter and the remaining scallops.

7. To serve, smooth the pea puree over a platter, top with the scallops, and drizzle with the Meyer lemon juice and about 3 tablespoons green oil. Top with the toasted pine nuts and the chives.

SERVES 4

PREP TIME
10 minutes

ACTIVE TIME
30 minutes

TOTAL TIME
40 minutes

MODERATE

When picking scallops, take a sniff— all you should smell is a slight scent of the salty sea. Too fishy? Skip 'em!

BRAISED BEEF BRISKET

WITH CARROTS AND TOMATOES

2 tablespoons canola oil

1 (4-pound) flat-cut brisket

Kosher salt and freshly ground black pepper

3 celery stalks, cut into 1-inch pieces

2 large yellow onions, cut into 1-inch pieces

2 large carrots, cut into 1-inch pieces

¼ cup water

4 garlic cloves, smashed

1 large bunch thyme, tied into a bundle with kitchen twine

2 cups dry red wine

1 (28-ounce) can whole peeled tomatoes, with juices

2 dried bay leaves, broken in half

1. Preheat the oven to 250°F.

2. In a large Dutch oven, heat the canola oil over medium-high heat. Liberally season the brisket all over with salt and pepper. Brown the brisket in the hot oil until a nice crust forms on both sides, about 5 minutes per side. Transfer to a large platter or baking sheet.

3. Add the celery, onions, carrots, water, and a pinch each of salt and pepper to the Dutch oven and cook, stirring occasionally, until lightly browned, 6 to 8 minutes. Add the garlic and the thyme bundle and cook, stirring occasionally, until the garlic is slightly tender, 2 minutes. Add the wine and cook until the wine has reduced by one-quarter, 4 to 5 minutes.

4. Squeeze and tear the tomatoes into small bits with your hands and add them to the pan, along with the juices from the can and the bay leaves. Bring to a boil over high heat, then nestle the brisket into the liquid (the liquid should come at least halfway up the brisket). Turn off the heat, cover the pot with a tight-fitting lid, and transfer it to the oven. Bake the brisket until a fork easily slips into the meat and the meat is tender but not falling apart, 3½ to 4 hours, flipping the meat halfway through.

5. Remove the pot from the oven and let the brisket rest in the pot for at least 15 minutes, then transfer it to a cutting board and slice it against the grain. Transfer the brisket slices to a large platter. Discard the thyme bundle and bay leaves from the sauce and vegetables. Season to taste, then pour the sauce and vegetables over the brisket and serve.

SERVES 8 TO 10

PREP TIME
15 minutes

ACTIVE TIME
35 minutes

TOTAL TIME
4½ to 5 hours
(includes braising and resting time)

EASY

Feel free to **make this in advance**; it tastes even better the next day.

ND

THANK
YOU
xx
David

MIXED GREENS
WITH FENNEL AND PINK GRAPEFRUIT

2 large Ruby Red grapefruits

1 large fennel bulb, fronds attached

1 tablespoon minced shallot

1½ teaspoons honey

1 tablespoon champagne vinegar

Kosher salt and freshly ground black pepper

¼ cup extra-virgin olive oil

About 4 ounces mixed baby greens

SPECIAL EQUIPMENT
mandoline

1. Slice both ends off each grapefruit. Stand one up and, following the curve of the fruit, cut away the peel and pith so the flesh is exposed. Hold the grapefruit over a bowl and use a paring knife to cut between the membrane of each segment to release the segments into the bowl. When you've cut out all the segments, squeeze the membrane over the bowl to extract even more juice, then discard the membrane. Set the grapefruit segments and 2 tablespoons of the juice aside (drink the rest or save it for another use!).

2. Separate the long stalks from the fennel bulb and discard them; set a few fennel fronds aside for serving. Halve the fennel bulb lengthwise and cut out the core. Place one fennel half cut-side down on a mandoline and slice it very thinly, following the grain of the vegetable; repeat with the remaining fennel half (you should have about 4 cups sliced fennel).

3. In a medium bowl, whisk together the shallot, honey, vinegar, reserved grapefruit juice, ½ teaspoon salt, and ¼ teaspoon pepper. While whisking, slowly stream in the olive oil until the dressing is creamy and emulsified.

4. In a large bowl, combine the fennel, mixed greens, ½ teaspoon salt, and a few hefty splashes of the dressing and toss to combine. Taste and season with additional salt.

5. Turn the salad out onto a large serving platter. Top with the grapefruit segments and reserved fennel fronds, and season with pepper. Serve immediately.

SERVES 4 TO 6

PREP TIME
5 minutes

ACTIVE TIME
20 minutes

TOTAL TIME
25 minutes

MODERATE

Swap in any citrus
you like here—blood oranges, clementines, and navel oranges all work great.

GRILLED BABY ARTICHOKES
WITH ZESTY VINAIGRETTE

Kosher salt and freshly ground black pepper

2 lemons

6 pounds baby artichokes (50 to 60)

½ cup extra-virgin olive oil

1 tablespoon Dijon mustard

¼ cup chopped fresh chives

¼ cup finely chopped fresh mint leaves

1 teaspoon red pepper flakes

Allium blossoms, for garnish (optional)

SPECIAL EQUIPMENT
outdoor grill or grill pan

1. Heat an outdoor grill to high or heat a grill pan over high heat. Bring a large pot of heavily salted water to a boil (the water should taste like the sea).

2. Fill a large bowl with cold water. Halve one of the lemons and squeeze the juice into the water, then toss in the lemon halves, too.

3. Working with one artichoke at a time, trim off the tip of the stem and remove a couple of layers of the tough outer leaves until you get to the tender, lighter green leaves. Cut off ¾ inch from the pointy end of the artichoke, then use a vegetable peeler to trim around the base to remove any tough, dark green areas. Slice the artichoke in half lengthwise and place it in the lemony water to prevent browning. Repeat with the remaining artichokes. Once you have all the artichokes prepped, remove them from the lemon water and add them to the boiling water. Cook until a paring knife slips easily into the base of the artichoke, about 8 minutes. Drain the artichokes in a colander and transfer them to a baking sheet to cool.

4. While the artichokes cook, zest and juice the remaining lemon into a medium bowl (you should have about ¼ cup juice). While whisking, add the olive oil, Dijon mustard, 1½ teaspoons salt, and a few cracks of black pepper.

5. Once the artichokes are cool enough to handle, place them in a large bowl with half the vinaigrette and toss to combine. Use tongs to transfer them to the hot grill and cook them until dark grill marks appear, 1 to 2 minutes on each side. Use tongs to return the grilled artichokes to the bowl.

6. Whisk the chives, mint, and red pepper flakes into the remaining vinaigrette, then toss with the grilled artichokes. Transfer to a platter and serve warm, garnished with allium blossoms, if you like.

SERVES 12

PREP TIME
1 hour

ACTIVE TIME
20 minutes

TOTAL TIME
1 hour 30 minutes

MODERATE

Look for larger baby artichokes, since a lot gets carved away. It's a lot of labor, but worth it. Those purple flowers you see are allium (onion) blossoms—look for them at specialty grocers and farmers' markets.

FLOURLESS CHOCOLATE CAKE

WITH ALMOND WHIPPED CREAM

10 tablespoons (1¼ sticks) unsalted butter, plus more for greasing

½ cup good-quality bittersweet chocolate chips

½ cup good-quality semisweet chocolate chips

Kosher salt

5 large eggs, separated

⅔ cup sugar

Unsweetened cocoa powder, for topping

1 cup heavy cream

¼ teaspoon almond extract

1. Preheat the oven to 325°F. Butter a 9-inch round metal cake pan, then line the bottom with parchment paper trimmed to fit.

2. Fill a medium saucepan with 1 inch of water and bring it to a strong simmer over medium heat. In a heatproof medium bowl, combine the bittersweet and semisweet chocolate chips, butter, and a pinch of salt and set it over the simmering water (the bottom of the bowl shouldn't touch the water). Cook, stirring occasionally, until the chocolate has completely melted and the mixture is well combined, about 5 minutes. Turn off the heat, remove the bowl from the saucepan, and set the chocolate aside to cool slightly.

3. In the bowl of a stand mixer fitted with the whisk attachment (or in a large bowl using a handheld mixer), combine the egg yolks and ⅓ cup of the sugar. Whip on medium speed until the mixture is slightly thick and forms ribbons when you lift the whisk out of the bowl, about 5 minutes. Add the chocolate mixture and beat until just combined. Pour the mixture into a separate large bowl and thoroughly clean and dry the mixer bowl and the whisk attachment.

4. Put the egg whites in the clean mixer bowl and beat on medium speed with the clean whisk attachment until foamy. Sprinkle with the remaining ⅓ cup sugar, then beat until the egg whites hold medium peaks, 4 to 5 minutes. Use a rubber spatula to fold the egg whites into the chocolate mixture until just combined. Do not overmix.

5. Pour the batter into the prepared cake pan, smooth and even out the top, and bake until the cake no longer jiggles when you tap the pan, 40 to 45 minutes. Set the pan on a wire rack and let cool completely, then run a small spatula or knife around the sides of the pan to release the cake. Using a sifter or fine-mesh sieve, sprinkle cocoa powder over the top of the cake.

SERVES 8 TO 10

PREP TIME
10 minutes

ACTIVE TIME
20 minutes

TOTAL TIME
1 hour 15 minutes

MODERATE

This is the **perfect** (*and* gluten-free!) dessert. Garnishing with cocoa powder instead of confectioners' sugar adds a dark-on-dark effect.

6. In the bowl of the stand mixer fitted with the whisk attachment, combine the cream and almond extract and beat until the cream holds medium peaks, 3 to 4 minutes.

7. Slice the cake and serve each slice with a generous dollop of the whipped cream.

WHOLLY HOLIDAY

(EASTER WITH A PASSOVER TWIST)

The arrival of sunny weather is reason enough to bring together family and close friends for a festive springtime meal, no matter what you're celebrating. Pick a neutral day that's not on anyone's actual holiday so all can celebrate together, and organize the event at your house or the home of a family member.

Growing up, while our Easter celebrations did have a more traditional feast with a leg of lamb and roast ham, what we kids looked forward to the most was the candy—lots and lots of candy. We also dyed eggs; my mom got really into it, creating ombré designs and all sorts of bells and whistles, while my dad would just dunk his eggs into every available color until the finished product was a lovely shade of…brown. These days, we try to make Easter special by taking the kids to a petting zoo or doing a traditional Easter egg hunt and, yes, lots and lots of candy. Hey—it's a family tradition!

WHAT GUESTS CAN BRING

Wine, a springy crudités-and-dip plate, cheese and crackers, and—most important—an appetite! Easter chocolate, matzo crackers, a flour-free Passover dessert.

GET GUESTS INVOLVED

Ask guests to make the quick yogurt sauce, dress the salad, shake the cocktails, put out the place cards, and hide the eggs.

WHAT TO WEAR

A spring dress, pastels, a seersucker suit, an Easter bonnet or hat.

THE TABLE

Lay out a runner of wheatgrass or fake AstroTurf. Cut place-mat shapes out of fresh moss sheets from the garden store. Use mix-and-match antique plates, silverware, and cloth napkins from your own collection or the thrift store—all in springy pastel shades.

THE FLOWERS

Tulips, daffodils, peonies. Accents of fresh herbs like thyme, lavender, and basil.

THE DRINKS

Signature cocktail from the menu, flat and sparkling water with mint and cucumber, regular and pink lemonade.

PLAN AHEAD

- *Three Days Before:* Make and freeze the cupcakes (but do not frost them). Make the apricot syrup. Shred cheese for the potatoes.
- *Two Days Before:* Make the French onion potatoes au gratin. Make the lemon-honey dressing. Chop the herbs for the lamb.
- *One Day Before:* Crust the lamb the night before. Peel the carrots. Caramelize the onions. Make the quick yogurt sauce.

HOST CRAFT PROJECT

Give out over-the-top Easter baskets for the kids, or organize an Easter egg hunt and hide a golden egg with a special surprise or money in it. Set out a station with matzo crackers, cream cheese frosting, and a variety of edible gel colors in tubes so kids can customize (and eat) their handiwork.

PARTY BASICS

Spring flowers, everything in shades of pastel, a nice table setting. Silverware and glasses that have been polished to their gleaming party best.

PARTY UPGRADES

Easter Learn how to fold a napkin in the shape of bunny ears. Line your centerpiece with jelly beans and marshmallow Peeps to make it colorful and Easter-like. Add accents of fake grass and colored eggs on the table. Take florist foam, cover it in wheatgrass, and nestle your flowers inside the florist foam to create a garden.

Passover Write everyone's names in Hebrew on matzo-backed place cards. Get Haggadah (Passover story) coloring books and crayons for the kids.

OVER-THE-TOP IDEAS

Make an Easter egg light garland by cutting holes in the tops of plastic eggs and fitting them over Christmas lights. Make stations for a cotton candy machine, ice cream booth, crafts, and face painting. Hire a petting zoo with baby farm animals, bunnies, baby chicks, and ducks. Hire an actor to come in an Easter bunny outfit and pass out candy and eggs to the kids.

PASSOVER CELEBRATION

- Since some people don't eat bread or flour on Passover, source the best gluten-free bread and desserts (flourless chocolate cake, anyone?) from a local bakery.
- Screen *The Ten Commandments*, the classic Hollywood Passover movie.
- Ask guests who observe Passover to bring a Haggadah, the book that tells the traditional Passover story of the exodus from slavery to freedom. Provide coloring versions for the kids.
- For flower arrangements, put together a spring bouquet. Then place matzos around the sides of square vases and tie all four sides of the crackers with a purple ribbon.
- Though bread crumbs are not kosher for Passover, you can swap matzo meal in most recipes for a holiday-friendly version.
- Everyone loves finding the *afikomen*—the broken piece of matzo that's hidden as part of the seder—so it could be fun to incorporate the tradition alongside the egg hunt. Put together some little prizes (like coloring books, stickers, or treats) for the kids (or grown-ups!) at your gathering—a first prize for whoever finds the *afikomen* and some runner-up goodies for the rest.

ACTIVITIES

An egg hunt (get a portable microphone and have a friend announce the play-by-play like a professional sportscaster). Set up Easter crafts; egg-and-spoon races; fill a giant bowl with jelly beans and guess how many there are. Play pin the tail on the bunny.

PARTY PROJECT

Make a bunny nose mask: Use ice pop sticks for the base, white pom-poms for the cheeks (and a smaller one for the nose), pipe cleaners for the whiskers, and two rectangular paper cutouts for the teeth.

GIFTS FOR GUESTS

For kids: Baskets filled with toys, candy, books, games, plush bunnies, and chicks.

For adults: A bottle of rosé, gourmet chocolate truffles, pastel nail polish, a ceramic bunny, a small plant, adult coloring books, and a spring-scented candle.

KEEP THE PARTY GOING

Screen *Easter Parade, Hop, Jesus Christ Superstar*, or *It's the Easter Beagle, Charlie Brown*, or play Easter bingo or Easter charades.

PLAYLIST

"**Easter,**" Patti Smith Group

"**Morning Has Broken,**" Yusuf/Cat Stevens

"**Rabbit Heart (Raise It Up),**" Florence + the Machine

"**Amazing Grace,**" Anne Murray

"**Put on Your Sunday Clothes,**" from *Hello, Dolly!* Gavin Creel and Bette Midler

"**Easter Song,**" Keith Green

"**Superstar,**" from *Jesus Christ Superstar*, original Broadway cast recording

"**Easter Parade,**" Judy Garland

"**Do You Know Him?**" Mahalia Jackson

"**Rise,**" Katy Perry

"**When I Get Where I'm Going,**" Brad Paisley and Dolly Parton

"**Oh Happy Day,**" Aretha Franklin and Mavis Staples

"**What a Wonderful World,**" Louis Armstrong

LILLET AND APRICOT COCKTAIL

FOR THE APRICOT SIMPLE SYRUP

6 fresh apricots, halved and pitted, or 6 ounces dried apricots, halved (about 1 heaping cup)

2 cups sugar

2 cups water

FOR THE COCKTAIL

1 lemon

Ice

10 ounces Lillet Blanc

2 ounces vodka

6 to 8 ounces lemon seltzer (such as Bubly)

1. To make the apricot simple syrup using fresh apricots: Place the apricots in a heatproof medium bowl and set aside. In a medium saucepan, combine the sugar and water and bring to a boil, stirring until the sugar has completely dissolved. Pour the hot simple syrup over the apricots and let steep for 1 hour. (You should get about 3 cups syrup.) Strain the simple syrup through a fine-mesh sieve, reserving the apricot halves for garnish.

To make the apricot simple syrup using dried apricots: In a medium saucepan, combine the dried apricots, sugar, and water and bring to a boil, stirring until the sugar has completely dissolved. Reduce the heat to medium-low and simmer for 5 minutes more. Turn off the heat and let the syrup cool to room temperature. (The simple syrup and apricots can also be refrigerated, covered, for up to 1 week to deepen the flavor of the syrup.)

2. Make the cocktail: Using a channel zester or peeler, cut twists from the lemon rind and set aside. Juice the lemon and strain out the seeds.

3. Fill two rocks glasses with crushed ice. In a shaker, combine 6 ice cubes, the Lillet, ¼ cup of the apricot syrup, the vodka, and 2 tablespoons of the lemon juice. Shake vigorously, pour into the prepared glasses, and top off with lemon seltzer. Garnish with a lemon twist and a soaked apricot.

MAKES 2 DRINKS

PREP TIME
15 minutes

ACTIVE TIME
10 minutes

TOTAL TIME
1 hour 30 minutes

EASY

ENDIVE AND CELERY SALAD

WITH LEMON-HONEY DRESSING

The lemon-honey dressing, the crunch of the hazelnuts, and the light and fresh endive make for a great combination in this addictive salad.

1 teaspoon finely grated lemon zest

2 tablespoons lemon juice (from ½ lemon)

1 tablespoon Dijon mustard

1 tablespoon honey

Kosher salt and freshly ground black pepper

¼ cup extra-virgin olive oil

4 or 5 medium endive heads, cored and cut into ½-inch-thick pieces (about 4 cups)

7 celery stalks, with leaves, sliced ¼ inch thick on an angle

½ cup hazelnuts, toasted and coarsely chopped

1. In a large bowl, whisk together the lemon zest, lemon juice, mustard, honey, and a large pinch each of salt and pepper. While whisking, slowly stream in the olive oil until the vinaigrette is creamy and emulsified (this can be done ahead of time; re-whisk if needed to combine just before serving).

2. Add the endive and celery to the bowl and toss gently to combine. Taste and season with salt and pepper. Add half the hazelnuts and toss to incorporate, then transfer the mixture to a serving bowl and serve topped with the remaining hazelnuts.

SERVES 4 TO 6

PREP TIME
20 minutes

ACTIVE TIME
5 minutes

TOTAL TIME
25 minutes

EASY

Feel free to swap in walnuts or pecans for the hazelnuts.

ROAST LEG OF LAMB

¼ cup finely chopped fresh oregano

¼ cup finely chopped fresh rosemary

¼ cup finely chopped fresh thyme

3 tablespoons minced garlic (about 6 large cloves)

¼ cup Dijon mustard

¼ cup olive oil

1 tablespoon kosher salt

1 teaspoon freshly ground black pepper

1 (7- to 8-pound) bone-in leg of lamb, tied (Have your butcher do this.)

Halved pitted apricots, for garnish

Chopped fresh mint, for garnish

SPECIAL EQUIPMENT
instant-read thermometer

QUICK
YOGURT SAUCE

Makes about 2 cups

2 cups Greek yogurt
1 cup chopped mint
Zest and juice of 1 lemon
1 tablespoon extra-virgin olive oil
Kosher salt and freshly ground
black pepper

Whisk together the
ingredients and season with
salt and pepper to taste.

1. In a small bowl, stir together the oregano, rosemary, thyme, garlic, Dijon mustard, olive oil, salt, and pepper. Set the lamb on a cutting board and rub the paste all over, then lightly enclose it in plastic wrap and refrigerate for at least 8 hours and up to 24 hours.

2. Preheat the oven to 450°F.

3. Remove the lamb from the refrigerator, remove the plastic wrap, and place the lamb on a rack set in a large roasting pan. Let sit at room temperature for at least 30 minutes. Roast for 30 minutes, then reduce the oven temperature to 375°F and roast until an instant-read thermometer inserted into the thickest part of the lamb reads 135°F, about 1 hour 30 minutes more.

4. Remove the pan from the oven and let the lamb rest for 20 minutes before transferring it to a cutting board. Remove the butcher's twine and carve the lamb into thin pieces crosswise and against the grain, taking care to carve around the bone. Transfer to a platter and garnish with apricots and mint. Serve immediately with Quick Yogurt Sauce (see box).

SERVES 8 TO 10

PREP TIME
15 minutes

ACTIVE TIME
10 minutes

TOTAL TIME
10 hours
30 minutes
*(includes marinating,
roasting, and resting
time)*

EASY

◆

Got leftovers?
Slice them up for
gyros on the fly
the next day.

ASPARAGUS AND CARROTS

WITH BROWN BUTTER AND CHIVES

How can you go wrong with veggies in butter? Tarragon, parsley, or any other soft, tender herbs can replace the chervil, if needed.

Kosher salt and freshly ground black pepper

1 bunch small rainbow carrots (about 1 pound), chopped

2 pounds fresh asparagus, tough ends broken off, cut into 1-inch pieces (about 2 cups)

4 tablespoons (½ stick) unsalted butter

1 small shallot, finely chopped (about ¼ cup)

1 tablespoon packed light brown sugar

3 tablespoons red wine vinegar

¼ cup chopped fresh chervil

1. Bring a large saucepan of heavily salted water to a boil (the water should taste like the sea). Add the carrots and cook until crisp-tender, about 2 minutes. Use a slotted spoon to transfer the carrots to a baking sheet or large plate to cool.

2. Return the water to a boil, add the asparagus, and cook until crisp-tender, about 2 minutes. Drain the asparagus in a fine-mesh sieve and transfer to a large bowl to cool.

3. In a large skillet, melt the butter over medium-high heat, then cook the melted butter until there are visible chestnut brown flecks, about 2 minutes. Reduce the heat to medium-low, add the shallot, and cook, stirring often, until softened, about 1 minute. Whisk in the brown sugar and vinegar and cook until the sugar has dissolved, about 1 minute. Add the cooled asparagus and carrots and stir to combine. Cook until the vegetables are warmed through, about 1 minute.

4. Taste and season with salt and pepper. Stir in half the chervil and transfer to a serving bowl. Sprinkle with the remaining chervil and serve.

SERVES 6 TO 8

PREP TIME
15 minutes

ACTIVE TIME
10 minutes

TOTAL TIME
30 minutes

EASY

FRENCH ONION

POTATOES AU GRATIN

6 tablespoons canola oil, plus more for greasing

3 large onions (about 2¼ pounds), quartered and thinly sliced

Kosher salt and freshly ground black pepper

2 garlic cloves, minced

6 to 8 Yukon Gold potatoes (about 2½ pounds), peeled and very thinly sliced

12 ounces Gruyère cheese, shredded

2½ cups half-and-half

1. In a large straight-sided skillet, heat the canola oil over medium heat. Add the onions and a large pinch each of salt and pepper and cook, stirring occasionally, until the onions are sticky, tender, browned, and nearly jammy, about 1 hour. If the onions stick to the pan at any time, add a tablespoon of water and use a wooden spoon or heatproof spatula to scrape up any browned bits from the bottom of the pan.

2. Stir in the garlic and cook, stirring occasionally, until fragrant, about 5 minutes. Turn off the heat and let the caramelized onions cool slightly. (The caramelized onions can be made the day before and stored in an airtight container in the refrigerator.)

3. Preheat the oven to 400°F. Brush a 9 by 13-inch baking dish with canola oil.

4. Lay one-fifth of the potatoes over the bottom of the pan. Season the potatoes with ½ teaspoon salt and a pinch of pepper. Sprinkle with one-fifth of the caramelized onions, followed by one-fifth of the Gruyère, then pour ½ cup of the half-and-half over the cheese. Repeat this process four more times.

5. Place the baking dish on a large baking sheet and bake until a wooden skewer inserted into the middle meets no resistance and the top is bubbling and browned, about 1 hour 30 minutes, rotating the pan halfway through the cooking time.

6. Remove from the oven and let sit for at least 20 minutes and up to 1 hour to solidify before slicing into pieces and serving.

SERVES 8 TO 10

PREP TIME
20 minutes

ACTIVE TIME
15 minutes

TOTAL TIME
3 hours
50 minutes

EASY

Let these sit for an hour post-baking; not only will the flavors meld, but the potatoes will firm up as they cool, making them easier to serve.

COCONUT CUPCAKES

WITH COCONUT BUTTERCREAM FROSTING

1 (13.6-ounce) can full-fat, unsweetened coconut milk, whisked until smooth

½ cup buttermilk

3 cups all-purpose flour

1 teaspoon baking powder

½ teaspoon baking soda

Kosher salt

3½ cups (7 sticks) unsalted butter, at room temperature

2 cups granulated sugar

5 large eggs

5 cups sweetened flaked coconut

3¾ cups confectioners' sugar (about 1 pound), sifted

Green food dye, as needed

Miniature candy-coated milk chocolate eggs and/or your favorite Easter candies, as needed

Tip *These cupcakes can even be made a few weeks ahead and stored (unfrosted) in the freezer! After baking, let them cool completely, then store them in a single layer in zip-top bags in the freezer. The night before the party, leave them on the counter to defrost, then prepare the frosting and frost them as usual before the guests arrive.*

1. Preheat the oven to 325°F. Line two 12-cup muffin tins with paper liners.

2. In a small bowl, whisk together ½ cup of the coconut milk and the buttermilk and set aside. In a separate medium bowl, whisk together the flour, baking powder, baking soda, and ½ teaspoon salt and set aside.

3. In the bowl of a stand mixer fitted with the paddle attachment (or in a large bowl if using a handheld mixer), cream 1½ cups (3 sticks) of the butter and the granulated sugar on high speed until light and fluffy, about 5 minutes, scraping the sides of the bowl with a rubber spatula as needed. Reduce the speed to medium-low and add the eggs one at a time, mixing well after each addition and scraping the sides of the bowl as needed. With the mixer on low speed, add one-third of the flour mixture. Mix until just combined, then add half the buttermilk mixture and mix until just combined. Repeat with the remaining flour and buttermilk mixtures, then fold in 2 cups of the flaked coconut.

4. Fill each prepared muffin cup three-quarters full with batter and set the tins side by side on the middle rack in the oven. Bake until a cake tester inserted into the center of a cupcake comes out clean and the tops are very lightly browned, 20 to 25 minutes, rotating the tins after 15 minutes. Remove from the oven and let the cupcakes cool in the tins for 20 minutes, then transfer them to a wire rack to cool completely.

5. Clean the mixer bowl and fit the mixer with the whisk attachment. In the mixer bowl, combine the remaining 2 cups (4 sticks) butter, the remaining coconut milk, and a pinch of salt and beat on medium speed until completely combined. (The mixture might initially look curdled but will come together as you beat it.) Increase the speed to high and beat until light and fluffy, about 5 minutes. Reduce the speed to medium-low and add the confectioners' sugar in two additional batches, scraping down the bowl as needed.

MAKES 24 CUPCAKES

PREP TIME
15 minutes

ACTIVE TIME
40 minutes

TOTAL TIME
1 hour 40 minutes

MODERATE

Although I've garnished them with seasonal treats here, these are **year-round winners**—top them as you wish.

Increase the speed to high and whip until light and fluffy, 2 to 4 minutes. If desired, mix 8 drops of the green dye into the frosting for a pale shade of green; add additional green dye if you want a stronger color. Fold in 2 cups of the flaked coconut. Set the frosting aside.

6. Put the remaining 1 cup flaked coconut in a small bowl and, with either gloved hands or a fork, mix in 6 to 8 drops of green dye until the coconut resembles cut grass. Add additional green dye if needed.

7. Use a butter knife to frost the cooled cupcakes with the frosting, then sprinkle them with the flaked coconut. Decorate the tops with Easter candies as desired.

MEXICAN FIESTA

Spring means fiesta time for you and your friends—what could be better than a fresh-air feast where the food, décor, and activities scream "fun, fun, fun"? This can be any time, though it would be particularly well suited for a Cinco de Mayo celebration—preferably outside, if the weather is nice. This gathering plan contains a piñata's worth of ideas for delicious Mexican-inspired cocktails and eats that will get the party started…and keep it going until the last *olé!*

WHAT GUESTS CAN BRING

Tortilla chips, their favorite salsas, Mexican sodas, a piñata (or candy to fill one), fresh tropical fruits and veggies (jicama, pineapple, mango), Mexican candy.

GET GUESTS INVOLVED

Have guests mix the guacamole, set out tortilla chips, fill the salsa bowls, and shake the drinks.

WHAT TO WEAR

Bright colors like red, pink, black, yellow, turquoise, bright blue, and green. The colors of the Mexican flag (green, red, and white). Embroidered peasant tops and dresses.

THE TABLE

Lay colorful striped Mexican-style runner or blanket on the table. Collect clean old cans from Mexican food items (Goya beans, salsa, coconut milk, chili) and fill them with brightly colored flowers. Use Fiestaware (there's lots available online) and candles.

THE FLOWERS

Brightly colored dahlias, ranunculus, Gerbera daisies, cacti, succulents.

THE DRINKS

Lots of Mexican beer like Corona, Dos Equis, and Negro Modelo; Jarritos (Mexican sodas in flavors like hibiscus, watermelon, and lime); horchata (a traditional sweetened almond drink); water.

PLAN AHEAD

- *Three Days Before:* Bake the chile-chocolate cookies and freeze them.
- *Two Days Before:* Assemble, bake, and refrigerate the green chile enchiladas.
- *One Day Before:* Prepare all the elements for the guacamole except the avocados themselves. Make your aguas frescas. Set the table and make tissues-paper Mexican flowers.

PARTY BASICS

Lots of beer and margarita mix, brightly colored decorations, a Mexican flag, fans, maracas, a candle set in the center of a bowl surrounded by chile peppers (or thread chiles onto string and hang them).

PARTY UPGRADES

A piñata, paper *picados* (laser-cut banners), Mexican wrestling masks, big balloon letters that spell "fiesta" or "Cinco de Mayo." Vanilla-frosted cupcakes decorated with green and red sprinkles in the pattern of the Mexican flag.

OVER-THE-TOP IDEAS

Hire a mariachi band. Set up a margarita bar. Shape balloons into a cactus sculpture. Set up a fireworks display.

HOST CRAFT PROJECT

PAPER-CUT FLOWERS

Stack multicolored tissue paper, then fold it into an accordion-style fold about 1 inch thick. Staple the center (or tie it with a pipe cleaner), cut the edges into round or petal shapes, then unfold. Peel the layers toward the center, and voilà! You've got flowers you can now hang with pipe cleaners.

ACTIVITIES
Take pictures in a photo booth using Cinco de Mayo props; teach a Mexican dance to the crowd.

PARTY PROJECT
Have guests make Frida Kahlo–style headbands and decorate their own ponchos with fake flowers, using glue guns and various craft materials.

GIFTS FOR GUESTS
Mini stuffed piñatas, Red Hots, mini candy tacos.

KEEP THE PARTY GOING
Screen Coco, *Three Amigos*, *Frida*, or *Y Tu Mamá También*.

PLAYLIST

"**Oye Como Va**," Santana

"**Cinco De Mayo**," War

"**Señorita**," Justin Timberlake

"**Bidi Bidi Bom Bom**," Selena

"**Me Voy a Ir**," Jenny and the Mexicats

"**Bailando**," Enrique Iglesias

"**Loca**," Shakira

"**Amor a la Mexicana**," Thalía

"**México Lindo y Querido**," Vicente Fernández

"**Na Na Na (Dulce Niña)**," A. B. Quintanilla II

"**Fun in Acapulco**," Elvis Presley

"**Amor, Amor, Amor**," Jennifer Lopez

CLASSIC MARGARITA

Ice

4 ounces blanco tequila

1½ ounces good-quality triple sec, such as Combier or Cointreau

3 tablespoons fresh lime juice (about 1 large lime)

1 tablespoon simple syrup (see page 9)

2 lime wedges, for garnish

Kosher salt

A classic marg doesn't use simple syrup, but I like a sweet splash in mine. Since this recipe has only five main ingredients, don't skimp on quality: Always use fresh lime juice, and invest in a top-shelf triple sec such as Combier or Cointreau.

1. Fill a cocktail shaker to the top with ice, then add the tequila, triple sec, lime juice, and simple syrup. Shake like crazy, then strain into two rocks glasses filled with fresh ice.

2. Dip a lime wedge halfway into salt, then make a shallow cut in the wedge and perch it on the rim of the glass. Repeat with another lime wedge for the second glass. Serve immediately.

MAKES 2 DRINKS

PREP TIME
5 minutes

ACTIVE TIME
5 minutes

TOTAL TIME
10 minutes

EASY

These are done in **single portions**, but you can easily make them in **larger batches**.

AGUAS FRESCAS

We first discovered these refreshing drinks in Mexico, where they're as ubiquitous as soda is in the US. The mango and watermelon flavors are more traditional; my cucumber-matcha version is a refreshing, not-too-sweet pick-me-up.

For each agua fresca, combine all the ingredients in a blender and blend until smooth. You should have about 3 cups of each flavor. Chill for at least 1 hour 30 minutes, or up to 3 days, covered, before serving over ice.

FOR THE WATERMELON AGUA FRESCA

2 cups cubed seedless watermelon

1½ cups water

2 tablespoons sugar

2 tablespoons fresh lime juice

FOR THE MANGO AGUA FRESCA

1 cup cubed mango

2¼ cups water

1 tablespoon sugar

2 tablespoons fresh lime juice

FOR THE CUCUMBER–MATCHA AGUA FRESCA

2 cups cubed peeled English cucumber (about 1 medium)

2 teaspoons matcha powder

1½ cups water

3 tablespoons sugar

2 tablespoons fresh lime juice

Ice

MAKES 4 DRINKS
of each flavor
—
12 drinks total

PREP TIME
15 minutes

ACTIVE TIME
10 minutes

TOTAL TIME
2 hours (includes chilling time)

EASY

◆

Fill your **piñata** with authentic **Mexican candy** and small **toys**.

GUACAMOLE

In the lemon vs. lime guacamole debate, I come down on the side of lemons; they just give the guac more zip. Besides, I got the idea from Ina Garten, the undisputed queen of everything cooking-related. If it's good enough for Ina, it's good enough for me!

6 ripe avocados, halved, pitted, and peeled

Juice of 1 large lemon (about ¼ cup)

1 garlic clove, finely grated on a Microplane

1 small red onion, finely diced (about 1 cup)

2 tablespoons finely chopped fresh cilantro, plus whole leaves for garnish

Kosher salt and freshly ground black pepper

1 jalapeño, finely minced

2 Roma (plum) tomatoes, halved, seeded, and cut into ¼-inch pieces

Hot sauce

Tortilla chips, store-bought or homemade (see page 66)

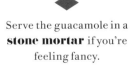

Serve the guacamole in a **stone mortar** if you're feeling fancy.

1. In a medium bowl, use your hands to mash the avocados with the lemon juice, garlic, red onion, cilantro, and a large pinch each of salt and pepper. (Or have your kids mash up the avocado with their hands first. Kids love getting their hands dirty.) Wash your hands, then use a spoon or spatula to stir in the jalapeño, half the tomatoes, and hot sauce to taste. Taste the guacamole and season with salt and pepper.

2. Transfer the guacamole to a serving bowl and garnish with the rest of the tomatoes and the whole cilantro leaves. Serve immediately with tortilla chips. Transfer any leftover guacamole to an airtight container and nestle an avocado pit into the guacamole to prevent browning. Press plastic wrap directly onto the surface of the guacamole and seal the container. Store in the refrigerator and eat within 1 day.

SERVES 6 TO 8

PREP TIME
10 minutes

ACTIVE TIME
5 minutes

TOTAL TIME
15 minutes

EASY

**Save at least
one avocado pit**
to nestle into any
leftover guacamole;
this helps keep it from
browning!

RED SNAPPER AND SHRIMP

CEVICHE

There are no rules in this dish—the only given is that it's healthy, clean, and refreshing. If you want to add red peppers instead of the jalapeños, go for it!

1 medium red onion, thinly sliced (about 1¼ cups)

1 cup fresh lime juice (from 6 to 8 limes)

1 jalapeño, seeded (if you want less heat) and minced

1 garlic clove, finely grated on a Microplane

Kosher salt

1 pound skinless red snapper fillets, cut into ⅓-inch dice

1 cup chopped fresh cilantro, plus whole leaves for garnish

1 pound (16 to 20) raw shrimp, peeled and deveined

1 English cucumber, skin peeled into stripes, seeded, and finely diced (about 2 cups)

4 small Roma (plum) tomatoes, seeded and finely chopped (about 2 cups)

2 tablespoons extra-virgin olive oil

Homemade Tortilla Chips (recipe follows)

1. In a large glass bowl, stir together the red onion, lime juice, jalapeño, garlic, and 1 teaspoon salt. Add the snapper and cilantro and stir gently to combine. Cover and refrigerate until the fish is opaque and just "cooked" through, at least 4 hours but no more than 6 hours (in ceviche the citric acid in the lime juice breaks down, or denatures, the fish in a way similar to cooking with heat).

2. Meanwhile, bring a small saucepan of lightly salted water to a boil. Line a small baking sheet with parchment paper. Stir the shrimp into the boiling water, turn off the heat, cover, and let stand for 2 minutes. Drain the shrimp, then place them in a single layer on the prepared baking sheet and freeze until the shrimp are cool to the touch, about 10 minutes (this stops them from overcooking). Cut the cooled shrimp into ⅓-inch pieces and transfer to a small bowl; cover and refrigerate until ready to serve.

3. When ready to serve, gently stir the shrimp, cucumber, tomatoes, and olive oil into the snapper mixture. Taste and season with additional salt. Transfer to a large serving bowl and garnish with cilantro leaves. Serve immediately with tortilla chips.

RECIPE CONTINUES

SERVES
6 TO 8

makes about
6 cups

PREP TIME
25 minutes

ACTIVE TIME
30 minutes

TOTAL TIME
4 hours to
6 hours 30
minutes (includes
refrigeration time)

EASY

Homemade Tortilla Chips

Makes 60 chips, 6 to 8 servings ◆ *Prep time:* 5 minutes
Active time: 10 minutes ◆ *Total time:* 10 minutes

Canola oil, for frying

12 (6-inch) corn tortillas, each cut into 5 long strips

Kosher salt

SPECIAL EQUIPMENT
deep-fry thermometer

1. Fill a large Dutch oven halfway with canola oil. Heat the oil over medium-high heat until a deep-fry thermometer registers 350°F. Set a wire rack on a baking sheet and set it nearby.

2. Working in batches, add the cut tortillas to the hot oil and fry, stirring occasionally with a metal spider, until crisp and lightly browned, about 1 minute. If you want the tortillas to curl a bit, use the back of the spider to gently hold the tortillas down in the hot oil.

3. Transfer the fried tortillas to the rack and season liberally with salt while they're hot. Serve still slightly warm or at room temperature. Store any leftover tortilla chips in an airtight container at room temperature for up to 1 week.

CHICKEN ENCHILADAS

This dish is an homage to Neil's roots in New Mexico, the land of hot green chiles. I make sure to have a tray of these in the freezer at all times; when he gets home after a trip I just pop them into the oven, garnish with cilantro and pickled onions—and it's his home state on a plate.

1 teaspoon cumin seeds

1 teaspoon coriander seeds

2 tablespoons canola oil, plus more for frying

1½ pounds boneless, skinless chicken thighs

Kosher salt

1 large yellow onion, diced (about 1½ cups)

4 garlic cloves, minced

12 ounces tomatillos, husks removed, rinsed well, and finely diced (about 2 cups)

2 (4-ounce) cans mild or hot diced Hatch chiles, undrained

2 cups low-sodium chicken stock

1 dried bay leaf, halved crosswise

8 (6-inch) corn tortillas

1½ cups shredded Mexican cheese blend (6 ounces)

Mexican crema, for drizzling

Fresh cilantro leaves, for garnish

¼ cup Pickled Red Onions (recipe follows), for garnish

SPECIAL EQUIPMENT
spice grinder

1. In a small dry skillet, toast the cumin and coriander seeds over medium heat, stirring occasionally, until fragrant, about 3 minutes. Turn off the heat and transfer to a plate to cool completely, then grind in a spice grinder until fine.

2. In a large Dutch oven, heat the 2 tablespoons canola oil over medium-high heat until the oil starts to shimmer. Season the chicken liberally on both sides with salt. Working in batches if necessary, sear the chicken on both sides until light golden brown, 6 to 8 minutes total; transfer to a baking sheet or plate and reserve, leaving any fat in the pot.

3. Add the onion, a pinch of salt, and a splash of water to the Dutch oven and cook, stirring occasionally, until slightly softened and lightly browned, 6 to 8 minutes. Reduce the heat to medium, add the garlic, and cook until the garlic has softened, about 2 minutes. Stir in the toasted cumin and coriander, tomatillos, chiles, stock, and bay leaf.

4. Nestle the chicken into the liquid until mostly submerged. Increase the heat to medium-high, bring to a boil, then reduce the heat to maintain a simmer and cook, covered with the lid ajar, until the chicken is cooked through and very tender, about 30 minutes. Transfer the chicken to a plate or bowl and let cool.

5. Remove and discard the bay leaf halves and carefully blend the sauce directly in the pot with an immersion blender until completely smooth. (Alternatively, carefully transfer the sauce to a regular blender and blend until smooth.) Simmer the sauce over medium heat, uncovered, until it has reduced by one-quarter of its volume and thickened to a consistency similar to marinara sauce, about 20 minutes (there should be about 3 cups sauce left).

6. In a medium bowl, shred the chicken with two forks. Add ½ cup of the sauce and toss to coat. Taste and season with salt.

7. Preheat the oven to 375°F. Spread ½ cup of the sauce over the bottom of an 11 by 7-inch baking dish.

SERVES 4

PREP TIME
25 minutes

ACTIVE TIME
2 hours 10 minutes

TOTAL TIME
2 hours 10 minutes

MODERATE

RECIPE CONTINUES

8. Fill a large cast-iron skillet with canola oil to a depth of ½ inch and heat the oil over medium heat until it just starts to shimmer. Spoon 1 heaping cup of the sauce onto a rimmed medium plate. Working with one tortilla at a time, use a pair of tongs to quickly dip the tortilla into the hot oil just until it becomes malleable.

9. Drag both sides of the tortilla through the sauce on the plate, then place the tortilla on a clean work surface and let cool slightly. Spoon one-eighth of the chicken mixture down the center of the tortilla and sprinkle with 1½ teaspoons of the cheese.

10. Fold the tortilla over the chicken and cheese and roll it up so the filling stays snugly within the tortilla. Place the filled tortilla seam-side down in the baking dish and repeat with the remaining tortillas, chicken, filling, and cheese.

11. Spoon the remaining sauce evenly over the enchiladas and sprinkle with any remaining cheese. Bake until the sauce is bubbling and the cheese is lightly browned, about 20 minutes. Remove from the oven and let sit for 5 minutes before serving. Drizzle with the crema and garnish with the cilantro leaves and pickled red onions (about ¼ cup, but adjust to your liking).

Pickled Red Onions

Makes 3 cups ◆ *Prep time:* 5 minutes ◆ *Active time:* 10 minutes
Total time: 1 hour 10 minutes

1 large red onion, sliced into paper-thin rounds (about 2 cups)

1 tablespoon kosher salt

¼ cup sugar

1 cup red wine vinegar

¾ cup water

1. Put the sliced red onion in a heatproof medium glass bowl.

2. In a small saucepan, stir together the salt, sugar, vinegar, and water. Bring to a boil over medium-high heat and cook, stirring occasionally, until the sugar and salt have completely dissolved, about 5 minutes.

3. Pour the hot vinegar mixture over the onion and stir to combine; let cool completely, about 1 hour. Store in an airtight container in the refrigerator for up to 2 weeks.

ANCHO CHILE—MEXICAN CHOCOLATE

COOKIES

Neil's mom gave me a New Mexico cookbook, and these cookies were inspired by one of the recipes. There's just a little heat on the back end of every bite; calibrate the spiciness by using more or less of the chile powder to your liking.

1¾ cups all-purpose flour

⅓ cup good-quality unsweetened Dutch-process cocoa powder

2 teaspoons of your favorite ground chile powder, such as ancho chile

½ teaspoon baking soda

¼ teaspoon fine salt

¾ cup (1½ sticks) unsalted butter, at room temperature

1 cup packed dark brown sugar

½ cup granulated sugar

1 large egg

1½ teaspoons vanilla extract

1 cup dark chocolate chunks

½ cup unsalted pepitas (shelled pumpkin seeds), lightly toasted

1. Preheat the oven to 350°F. Line two large baking sheets with parchment paper.

2. In a medium bowl, whisk together the flour, cocoa powder, chile powder, baking soda, and salt. Set aside.

3. In the bowl of a stand mixer fitted with the paddle attachment, beat the butter on medium-high speed until light and creamy, about 1 minute. Add the brown sugar and granulated sugar and beat until slightly fluffy, about 2 minutes, scraping down the sides of the bowl with a rubber spatula as needed. Add the egg and vanilla and beat until well combined.

4. Reduce the mixer speed to medium-low; add half the flour mixture and beat until just combined, then add the remaining flour mixture and beat until the mixture just comes together, 1 to 2 minutes, being careful not to overmix. Add the chocolate chunks and pepitas and beat on low until just combined.

5. Use a 2-ounce ice cream scoop or a ¼-cup dry measuring cup to scoop the cookie dough onto the prepared baking sheets, making about 14 cookies total and leaving at least 2 inches between each cookie.

6. Bake until the edges of the cookies are crisp but the centers are still tender, about 15 minutes, rotating the baking sheets top to bottom and front to back halfway through the baking time. Remove from the oven, set the baking sheets on wire racks, and let the cookies cool completely on the pans. They should keep up to 5 days in an airtight container.

MAKES 14 COOKIES

PREP TIME
15 minutes

ACTIVE TIME
5 minutes

TOTAL TIME
30 minutes

EASY

SUMMER PICNIC

Fresh Blueberry Fizz 78
Fresh Mint Simple Syrup 78

Corn Cakes with Bacon Jam 80

Balsamic Cherry and Yogurt Parfaits with Olive Oil Granola 82
Balsamic Cherry Compote 82

Farro Salad with Grilled Asparagus, Crispy Mushrooms, and Whipped Ricotta 84

Pull-Apart Ham and Gruyère Sandwiches 86
Pull-Apart Parker House Rolls 87

Chocolate Chunk Hazelnut Bars 89

School's out for summer! Throw an afternoon brunch party to celebrate the warmth of summer and all the beauty it has to offer. Pop out a blanket wherever it strikes your fancy—your backyard, a neighborhood park, the beach, or somewhere under a shady tree.

PARTY BASICS

A portable speaker to play music and a mobile solar party charger. An umbrella for shade and sunscreen for sun. And don't forget your camera!

PARTY UPGRADES

Wooden boxes to set up the buffet, or small collapsible tables to create a multi-leveled presentation. Mason jars with flowers. Hula-hoops to see who can hoop the longest.

OVER-THE-TOP IDEAS

Bring a garland or pinwheels to hang from the trees around you. Bring bubbles, or binoculars for birdwatching.

WHAT GUESTS CAN BRING
Blankets or throws for the ground; wicker baskets filled with their own plates, napkins, and flatware. A cooler filled with water, drinks, and ice. An insulated coffee box, outdoor summer games (cornhole, potato sack race, ring toss), bug spray, sunscreen, and citronella candles. Also, garbage bags for cleanup.

GET GUESTS INVOLVED
Have people help look for the perfect picnic spot and help set up the blankets, games, food, and drinks. Ask someone to pick wildflowers for a centerpiece.

WHAT TO WEAR
Summer dresses, light fabrics to keep cool, and for the kids, clothes you won't mind getting dirty.

THE TABLE
In this case, more like a picnic blanket…but if you have a picnic table, even better! Red gingham tablecloths and canvas cloths are a plus. Bring a shower curtain to slip under your blanket to block any moisture in the ground. Use plastic or tin plates and easy-to-transport flatware. Upgrade from disposables—not only is it better for the environment, but it makes your event classier, too.

THE FLOWERS
Bring extra mason jars, send your kids on a wildflower-picking adventure, then give them the freedom to make sweet arrangements with what they find. Add easy summer flowers like daisies, sunflowers, black-eyed Susans, and marigolds into the mix.

THE DRINKS
Bring your own, water, soft drinks, rosé, Champagne, orange juice, and coffee (just make sure to check liquor laws before you drink alcohol in public spaces).

PLAN AHEAD
- *Three Days Before:* Make the bacon jam and the fresh mint simple syrup.
- *Two Days Before:* Make the granola and the cherry compote.
- *One Day Before:* Make the bars.

HOST CRAFT PROJECT
Bring a Fujifilm Instax instant camera to take pictures of you and your guests. Right when the picture comes out, write the date and your names into the picture with a sharp object before it fully exposes.

ACTIVITIES
Games like duck, duck, goose or red rover; pickup football, soccer, kickball, horseshoes, Frisbee, and kite flying.

PARTY PROJECT
Have everyone bring a few obscure ingredients or spices and a blindfold. Take turns tasting the items and guessing which is which. Make jewelry out of wildflowers by tying the stems together to form floral chains of varying lengths.

GIFTS FOR GUESTS
Make an extra batch of the chocolate chunk bars and send them home with a box of baked goods.

KEEP THE PARTY GOING
Play all the games you brought, or come up with more. Invite a person who plays the guitar, gather everyone around, and sing songs.

PLAYLIST

"Stoned Soul Picnic," Laura Nyro

"Summertime," Chloe Brisson

"Washed Out," Life of Leisure

"Dog Days Are Over," Florence + the Machine

"All Summer Long," Kid Rock

"Saturday in the Park," Chicago

"Sunny Afternoon," The Kinks

"Boogie in the Park," Joe Hill Louis

"Hot Fun in the Summertime," Sly and The Family Stone

"Steal My Sunshine," Len

"Rollin," Calvin Harris

"Easy," Real Estate

"In the Summertime," Mungo Jerry

FRESH BLUEBERRY FIZZ

½ cup fresh blueberries, plus
6 blueberries for garnish

¼ cup Fresh Mint Simple Syrup (recipe
follows)

4 ounces vodka

Ice

Splash of club soda

2 sprigs mint, for garnish

Put the blueberries in a cocktail shaker and use a cocktail muddler to crush them, then add the mint syrup, vodka, and enough ice to fill the shaker. Cover the shaker tightly with the top and shake vigorously for a few seconds, or until the mixture is very cold. Hold a mesh strainer over the top of the strainer on the shaker top and double-strain the cocktail into two lowball glasses filled with crushed ice; top each glass with a splash of club soda and garnish with a sprig of mint.

MAKES 2 DRINKS

PREP TIME
5 minutes

ACTIVE TIME
5 minutes

TOTAL TIME
5 minutes

EASY

FRESH BLUEBERRY FIZZ
MOCKTAIL
Substitute ½ cup lemonade
for the vodka.

Fresh Mint Simple Syrup

Makes 1 cup ◆ *Prep time:* 5 minutes ◆ *Active time:* 5 minutes
Total time: 1 hour 10 minutes (includes cooling time) ◆ *Easy*

¾ cup sugar

¾ cup water

1 large bunch fresh
mint (1 ounce)

1. In a small saucepan, stir together the sugar and water and bring to a simmer over medium heat. Cook, stirring, until the sugar has completely dissolved, 3 to 5 minutes.

2. Turn off the heat, then use your hands to tear the bunch of mint in half, add it to the saucepan, and use a spoon to press down on the mint to completely submerge it in the syrup. Let the syrup cool in the saucepan for 1 hour.

3. Set a fine-mesh strainer over a small bowl and pour in the syrup and mint. Strain the syrup, using the back of a spoon to press down on the mint to extract as much flavor as possible. The fresh mint simple syrup will keep in an airtight container in the refrigerator for up to 1 month.

CORN CAKES

WITH BACON JAM

FOR THE BACON JAM

1 pound bacon slices, cut crosswise into ¼-inch-wide pieces

1 large yellow onion, thinly sliced

2 tablespoons tomato paste

2 tablespoons packed dark brown sugar

¼ cup sherry vinegar

½ teaspoon red pepper flakes

Kosher salt

FOR THE CHIVE SOUR CREAM

½ cup sour cream

4 tablespoons sliced chives

FOR THE CORN CAKES

2 cups fresh corn kernels (from 2 to 3 large ears of corn)

2 tablespoons unsalted butter, melted and cooled slightly

2 large eggs, separated

⅓ cup stone-ground yellow cornmeal

⅓ cup all-purpose flour

1 tablespoon granulated sugar

1 teaspoon garlic powder

1 teaspoon kosher salt, plus more for seasoning

¼ teaspoon freshly ground black pepper, plus more for seasoning

1. Make the bacon jam: Place the bacon in a large cast-iron skillet and cook over medium heat, stirring often, until the fat has completely rendered and the bacon is crispy and deeply golden brown, about 25 minutes. There should be only about 2 tablespoons of rendered fat in the pan at any time; as the bacon cooks, carefully spoon the excess fat into a glass jar or bowl and set it aside. You'll use it later for frying. Use a slotted spoon to transfer the bacon to a large paper towel–lined plate to drain. Remove all but 2 tablespoons of the fat from the pan, if necessary, and return the pan to medium heat.

2. Add the onion and a splash of water to the pan. Use the back of a wooden spoon to scrape up any browned bits from the bottom of the pan, then cook until the onion is completely tender and golden brown, 30 to 40 minutes, adding more water as needed if the onion sticks or starts to burn.

3. Stir in the tomato paste, brown sugar, vinegar, and red pepper flakes and cook, stirring frequently, until the mixture is thick, about 5 minutes. Transfer the mixture (including the cooled bacon) to a food processor and pulse until thick and jammy, about 15 pulses. Transfer the mixture to a small bowl, taste, and season with salt. Cover with plastic wrap and set aside at room temperature while you make the corn cakes. (If you're making the jam in advance, store it in an airtight container in the fridge for up to 7 days.)

4. Make the chive sour cream: In a small bowl, stir together the sour cream and 2 tablespoons of the chives; cover with plastic wrap and refrigerate.

5. Make the corn cakes: In a blender, combine 1½ cups of the corn, the butter, and the egg yolks and blend until mostly smooth. In a large bowl, whisk together the cornmeal, flour, sugar, garlic powder, salt, and pepper. Form a well in the center, add the wet corn mixture, and stir until just combined.

MAKES 20 TO 24 SMALL CAKES and 2 cups jam

PREP TIME
20 minutes

ACTIVE TIME
40 minutes

TOTAL TIME
2 hours 10 minutes

MODERATE

Eat this jam in small doses, or your cholesterol might go through the roof! If you have leftover bacon jam, spread it on toast or sandwiches.

6. In a medium bowl, whisk the egg whites until stiff peaks form. Fold the egg whites, the remaining ½ cup corn, and the remaining 2 tablespoons chives into the batter.

7. In a large cast-iron skillet, heat 2 tablespoons of the reserved bacon fat over medium-high heat. When the fat starts to shimmer, drop about 8 heaping tablespoons of the batter into the pan, 1 tablespoon at a time, leaving enough space between them to allow them to expand and for easy flipping. Cook until the edges begin to set and the bottoms are lightly browned, about 2 minutes, then flip and cook until the second side is lightly browned and the corn cake is cooked through, about 2 minutes more. Transfer the corn cakes to a wire rack set over a baking sheet. Cook the remaining batter, adding more bacon fat to the pan if needed. (Leftover bacon fat can be stored in an airtight container in the refrigerator for up to 1 month, or use it to make Bacon Fat Popcorn, page 273.) If needed, season with salt and pepper to taste. Serve the corn cakes hot or at room temperature, topped with the bacon jam and chive sour cream.

BALSAMIC CHERRY AND YOGURT PARFAITS

WITH OLIVE OIL GRANOLA

FOR THE OLIVE OIL GRANOLA

½ cup pure maple syrup

⅓ cup olive oil

1 teaspoon kosher salt

2 tablespoons millet

⅔ cup raw pepitas (shelled pumpkin seeds)

⅔ cup raw pecans, chopped

⅔ cup raw sliced almonds

1¼ cups untoasted unsweetened coconut chips

2¾ cups old-fashioned rolled oats

Balsamic Cherry Compote (recipe follows)

4 cups Greek yogurt, for serving

1. Make the granola: Preheat the oven to 275°F. Line a large baking sheet with parchment paper.

2. In a medium bowl, whisk together the maple syrup, olive oil, and salt. In a large bowl, combine the millet, pepitas, pecans, almonds, coconut chips, and oats. Pour the maple syrup mixture over the oat mixture and use your hands to combine. Evenly spread the granola mixture over the prepared baking sheet and bake until the granola is completely dry and the coconut is lightly browned around the edges, 1 hour 30 minutes to 2 hours, stirring every 15 minutes. Remove from the oven and let the granola cool completely on the baking sheet.

3. While the granola is baking, make the balsamic cherry compote.

4. To assemble the parfaits: In 8-ounce mason jars, build layers of Greek yogurt, then granola, then cherry compote, until full, finishing with a layer of granola. Repeat to assemble the additional parfaits. Serve immediately, or put lids on the jars, refrigerate, and serve within 3 hours. Store the leftover granola in an airtight container at room temperature for up to 1 month; serve over ice cream or snack on out of hand.

SERVES 8
—
makes 5 cups granola, with leftovers

PREP TIME
15 minutes

ACTIVE TIME
15 minutes

TOTAL TIME
2 hours 55 minutes

EASY

Make a double batch of this granola; not only is it delicious, but when packed in decorative bags or cellophane, it's a **perfect host gift**.

Balsamic Cherry Compote

Makes 1 quart compote

3 pounds cherries, stemmed and pitted (about 8 cups)

¼ cup balsamic vinegar

¼ cup pure maple syrup

Kosher salt and freshly ground black pepper

In a large saucepan, stir together the cherries, vinegar, maple syrup, and a pinch each of salt and pepper. Cook over medium-low heat, stirring occasionally, until the cherries are softened and completely submerged in a syrupy sauce, about 25 minutes. Transfer to a bowl and let cool completely (the compote will thicken as it cools).

FARRO SALAD

WITH GRILLED ASPARAGUS, CRISPY MUSHROOMS, AND WHIPPED RICOTTA

This super-flavorful salad is as gorgeous as it is delicious. Replace the farro with cooked wheat berries, barley, rice, or brown rice. The honey in the ricotta lends subtle sweetness; if you also like a kick, add some red pepper flakes.

Kosher salt

FOR THE FARRO SALAD

1 ounce dried porcini or morel mushrooms, or a combination

8 cups mixed fresh mushrooms, such as shiitake, cremini, and oyster, cleaned and trimmed

1 cup olive oil

2 teaspoons kosher salt

1/4 teaspoon freshly ground black pepper

6 garlic cloves, unpeeled

6 sprigs thyme

2 cups farro

1 pound spring onions or green garlic, halved If larger than a golf ball

1 pound asparagus, tough ends snapped off

1/4 cup chopped fresh flat-leaf parsley

1. Preheat the oven to 375°F. Heat an outdoor grill to medium-high or heat a grill pan over medium-high heat. Bring a large pot of heavily salted water to a boil (the water should taste like the sea). In another pot, bring 3 cups unsalted water to a boil.

2. **Make the farro salad:** Place the dried mushrooms in a medium bowl. Pour the unsalted boiling water over them and set aside to soak for 20 minutes. Remove the mushrooms from the soaking liquid and set aside; when they are cool enough to handle, chop into small pieces. Strain the soaking liquid through a coffee filter to remove any grit, then set aside as well.

3. Slice the fresh mushrooms into 1/2-inch-thick pieces and put them in a large bowl. Add 3/4 cup of the olive oil, 1 teaspoon of the kosher salt, and the pepper. Distribute the mushrooms evenly over a baking sheet and nestle the garlic cloves among them. Top with the thyme sprigs, spacing them evenly over the mushrooms. Roast, stirring occasionally, for 20 minutes. Remove from the oven and mix in the chopped reconstituted dried mushrooms, making sure to coat them with some of the oil from the baking pan. Return to the oven and roast until the mushrooms are evenly crispy, 20 to 25 minutes more.

4. Meanwhile, add the farro and the reserved mushroom soaking liquid to the salted boiling water, return the water to a boil, and cook until the grains are tender but still chewy and beginning to burst, about 18 minutes. Drain, transfer to a large bowl, and set aside to cool.

5. In a large bowl, toss the spring onions, asparagus, the remaining 1/4 cup olive oil, and the remaining 1 teaspoon kosher salt. Grill until a light char develops, about 3 minutes per side, then chop the asparagus into 1-inch pieces and the spring onions into 1/2-inch pieces; add the grilled vegetables to the bowl with the farro.

SERVES 12

PREP TIME
20 minutes

ACTIVE TIME
15 minutes

TOTAL TIME
1 hour 15 minutes

MODERATE

1½ teaspoons plus a pinch kosher salt

⅓ cup extra-virgin olive oil

2 teaspoons Dijon mustard

Grated zest of 2 lemons

Juice of 1½ lemons, plus more to taste

1 cup ricotta cheese

1 tablespoon honey

2 tablespoons extra-virgin olive oil

¼ teaspoon kosher salt

½ teaspoon freshly ground black pepper

outdoor grill or grill pan

6. Remove the roasted mushrooms from the oven and discard the thyme sprigs. Let cool slightly, then retrieve the garlic cloves and set them aside. Add the mushrooms and any oil from the baking sheet directly to the bowl with the farro. Stir in the chopped parsley.

7. Make the dressing: Squeeze the roasted garlic cloves out of their skins onto a cutting board, sprinkle with a pinch of salt, and smash them into a paste with the flat side of a knife. Transfer the paste to a small bowl and whisk in the olive oil, mustard, remaining salt, lemon zest, and lemon juice.

8. Make the whipped ricotta: In a medium bowl, whisk together the ricotta, honey, olive oil, kosher salt, and pepper until smooth.

9. Pour the dressing over the farro salad and toss to coat evenly. Serve family-style, topped with large dollops of the whipped ricotta.

HAM AND GRUYÈRE SANDWICHES

24 (2-inch-square) Pull-Apart Parker House Rolls (recipe follows)

3 tablespoons Dijon mustard

12 ounces Gruyère or other Swiss cheese, grated (about 3 cups)

12 ounces smoked ham, thickly sliced and chopped into ½-inch pieces

½ cup cornichons, sliced into thin rounds

4 tablespoons (½ stick) unsalted butter, at room temperature

1 teaspoon Worcestershire sauce

2 teaspoons dried minced onion

1. Preheat the oven to 350°F.

2. Slice the entire sheet of rolls in half without separating the individual rolls from one another. Spread 2 tablespoons of the mustard over the cut side of the tops of the rolls and set aside. Place the connected bottom rolls in a 9 by 13-inch baking dish (they should fit snugly). Sprinkle half the cheese over the rolls in an even layer.

3. Distribute the ham over the cheese, then sprinkle the cornichons evenly over the ham, followed by the remaining cheese. Complete the sandwiches by placing the tops of the rolls in the pan, mustard-side down, lining up the tops and the bottoms of the rolls.

4. In a small bowl, stir together the butter, the remaining 1 tablespoon mustard, and the Worcestershire sauce until blended. Use a spatula to spread the butter mixture evenly over the tops of the rolls in the pan, then sprinkle a little of the dried minced onion on top of each roll.

5. Cover the baking dish tightly with aluminum foil and bake until the cheese has melted, about 30 minutes. Remove the foil and bake until the bread begins to get toasty, about 10 minutes more. The sandwiches can be served hot (wait for the pan to cool down a bit, though), but are equally fantastic served at room temperature on your picnic blanket, straight out of the baking dish.

MAKES 24 SLIDERS

PREP TIME
10 minutes

ACTIVE TIME
5 minutes

TOTAL TIME
1 hour

EASY

Making your own rolls makes these picnic-perfect sliders next-level, but **store-bought rolls work great, too**.

Pull-Apart Parker House Rolls

Makes 24 rolls ◆ *Prep time:* 10 minutes ◆ *Active time:* 25 minutes ◆
Total time: 3 hours 45 minutes (includes rising time) ◆ *Moderate*

1¼ cups whole milk

2¼ teaspoons (1 envelope) active dry yeast

1 large egg

2 tablespoons sugar

2 teaspoons kosher salt

½ cup (1 stick) unsalted butter, melted

3¾ cups all-purpose flour, plus more for dusting

1 teaspoon canola oil, for oiling the bowl

Flaky salt (optional)

1. In a small saucepan, heat the milk over medium-low heat until just barely warm, about 3 minutes, testing it with your finger to make sure the milk is not too hot. Pour it into a large bowl, sprinkle with the yeast, and let sit until the yeast is foamy, about 5 minutes.

2. Add the egg, sugar, kosher salt, and half the melted butter and whisk to combine, then add the flour and stir with a stiff spatula until evenly mixed. Turn the dough out onto a floured counter and knead until smooth, about 5 minutes.

3. Form the dough into a ball and place it in a large, lightly oiled bowl, turning the dough in the bowl to coat with oil on all sides. Cover with plastic wrap and let rise in a warm area of the kitchen until doubled in volume, about 1 hour 30 minutes.

4. Brush a 9 by 13-inch baking dish with some of the melted butter. Turn the dough out onto the counter, then punch it down and divide it into 4 equal pieces. Roll each piece into a log, cut each log crosswise into 6 equal pieces, then form each piece into a ball. Arrange the dough balls in the prepared baking dish in four rows of 6 rolls each and brush them with half the remaining butter. If you are serving the rolls on their own, sprinkle each ball with flaky salt. If you are using the rolls to make Pull-Apart Ham and Gruyère Sandwiches (opposite), omit the salt. Cover the dish with plastic wrap and let rise until the dough balls expand to fill the baking dish, about 1 hour.

5. During the last 15 minutes of rising time, preheat the oven to 350°F.

6. Uncover the rolls and bake until they are golden brown on top, about 30 minutes, rotating the dish halfway through. Remove from the oven, drizzle with the remaining melted butter, and let cool for 5 minutes before serving.

CHOCOLATE CHUNK
HAZELNUT BARS

These are a great make-ahead dessert. They are wonderfully moist and gooey the first day they are baked, then get slightly crispy the second day.

1 cup (2 sticks) cold salted butter, cut into ½-inch cubes, plus more for greasing

¼ teaspoon baking soda

1 teaspoon baking powder

2½ cups all-purpose flour

½ cup granulated sugar

¾ cup packed light brown sugar

2 large eggs, beaten

1 teaspoon vanilla extract

½ cup hazelnuts, toasted and lightly crushed

2 cups dark chocolate chunks

2 pints of your favorite vanilla ice cream (optional)

1. Preheat the oven to 350°F. Line a rimmed quarter-sheet pan or a 9 by 13-inch baking dish with parchment paper and rub the parchment with a light coating of butter.

2. In a medium bowl, whisk together the baking soda, baking powder, and flour and set aside.

3. In the bowl of a stand mixer fitted with the paddle attachment, beat the butter on medium-high speed until blended together into one large, smooth ball. Add the granulated sugar and brown sugar and beat until completely combined and the mixture has the texture of wet sand, scraping down the sides of the bowl with a rubber spatula as needed, about 2 minutes. Add the eggs and vanilla and beat until well combined (there may be pebble-size pieces of butter visible in the mixture, which is okay). Reduce the speed to medium-low, add half the flour mixture, and beat until just combined. Add the remaining flour mixture and beat until the dough just comes together, about 30 seconds. Reduce the speed to low, add the hazelnuts and chocolate chunks, and mix until just combined.

4. Transfer the dough to the prepared pan and use your hands or a rubber spatula to lightly press the dough evenly into the pan. Bake until the edges are lightly golden and the top is dry to the touch, 16 to 18 minutes, rotating the pan halfway through the baking time. Remove from the oven, set the pan on a wire rack, and cool completely (it's okay if it is slightly underbaked when it comes out of the oven; it will continue to firm up as it cools).

5. To serve, preheat the oven to 350°F. Using a bench scraper or straight-sided metal spatula, cut the cookie block into 24 equal bars. Place the pan in the oven and cook until the chocolate has melted and the cookie bars are warmed through, about 5 minutes. The cookie bars can also be removed from the pan and reheated in the microwave. Use a metal spatula to transfer the cookie bars onto individual plates, and serve with vanilla ice cream, if desired.

MAKES 24 BARS

PREP TIME
15 minutes

ACTIVE TIME
35 minutes

TOTAL TIME
35 minutes

EASY

These bars are at their best when they're nice and **soft** in the middle, so it's better to **err on the side of underbaking**.

FANCY 'CUE

After you put the kids down, relax under the stars with a grill-centric menu that's as elegant as it is outdoorsy. A smokin'-hot summer night calls for cocktails, close friends, and a prime sunset view from your backyard, or anywhere you can set up a grill.

PARTY BASICS

Make sure your table is truly a feast for the eyes, laden with flowers, gleaming wineglasses, polished silver, and pressed napkins.

PARTY UPGRADES

Slip a provocative TableTopic card under each place setting to jump-start an engaging conversation. Fill your tablescape with glorious stone fruits, grapes on the vine, berries, figs, and nuts for a dessert guests can help themselves to.

OVER-THE-TOP IDEAS

Set the whole party outside in the woods, and adorn your staging ground with chandeliers suspended from trees and a bevy of candles. Send guests home with fancy chocolates, or make extra porcini spice rub and package it in treat bags with the recipe attached.

WHAT GUESTS CAN BRING
Games to play after dinner, a nice bottle of red wine to go with the steak, a crowd-friendly appetizer (cheese, crackers, a crudités platter with dip).

GET GUESTS INVOLVED
Have people shake cocktails, help stuff the branzino, help stuff the figs, set the table, light candles, or just keep you company as you man (or woman) the grill.

WHAT TO WEAR
Light yet dressy summer clothes like long chinos, a collared shirt or polo, or a breezy dress will make this evening feel like a special occasion. Suggest that guests bring a light jacket or wrap in case you're eating outside at night and it gets chilly.

THE TABLE
Candles, candles, candles! Skip the electricity and opt to eat by the romantic light of flickering flames instead. Use a nice dark tablecloth for dramatic effect, then mix in a variety of woods and metals for contrast. Go over the top with votives, flowers, and summer fruits (preferably with their leaves attached) for your tablescape.

THE FLOWERS
Brightly colored dahlias, astilbes, coneflowers, and peonies. Reds, oranges, and burgundies convey a rich, romantic atmosphere.

THE DRINKS
Start with the Sbagliato Cocktail. For water, fill ice cube trays with edible flowers, or arrange slices of citrus on a baking sheet in a single layer, then freeze overnight to make unbelievably chic ice cubes. Italian Pinot Grigio, French Sauvignon Blanc, and white Bordeaux pair well with the fish. Go for a Californian Cabernet, a European Bordeaux, or an Argentinian Malbec to complement the rib eye.

INFUSED LIQUORS

Start with any clean, airtight mason jar. Pick your flavorings: fresh fruit, herbs or vegetables, dried spices, citrus peels, and coffee beans all work well (use herbs and spices sparingly, as their flavor is more concentrated). Wash and cut any fresh produce and place your flavoring ingredients in the jar. Fill the jar with the liquor of your choice and screw the lid on securely. Shake the jar a few times, then store in the refrigerator (if using fresh produce) or on the countertop for 1 week, shaking the jar a couple of times per day. Strain the liquor into a clean jar and discard the spent flavorings. Enjoy the infused liquor in your favorite cocktail. Store produce-based infusions in airtight containers in the fridge; others can be stored at room temperature (they should keep for a long time because of the alcohol, but discard if you spot any cloudy or moldy bits floating around after a while).

◆ SOME IDEAS ◆
Lemon and basil gin
Watermelon and mint vodka
Peach and blackberry bourbon
Serrano chile tequila
Vanilla bean and orange rum

GIFTS FOR GUESTS

Send guests home with a fragrant candle bearing a sticker custom-printed with the theme and date of the dinner. Have a flower station so guests can put together a bouquet to take home.

PLAYLIST

"Summer Madness," Kool & the Gang

"Suddenly Last Summer," The Motels

"Summer Breeze," Jason Mraz

"Summertime," Annie Lennox

"Your Summer Dream," The Beach Boys

"Buzzcut Season," Lorde

"Feeling Good," Nina Simone

"Fantasy," Alina Baraz featuring. Galimatias

"A Summer Song," Chad and Jeremy

"Endless Summer Nights," Richard Marx

"Lazy," Marilyn Monroe

"Up on the Roof," The Drifters

"Lovely Day," Bill Withers

PLAN AHEAD

- *Three Days Before:* Make the porcini rub.
- *Two Days Before:* Cut the vegetables for the grilled veggies, prep the cocktail components, and roast the tomatoes for the steak dish.
- *One Day Before:* Prep the herbs and lemon for the fish; marinate the vegetables you cut the day before.

HOST CRAFT PROJECT

Craft your own limoncello using lemon rinds, sugar, and vodka or distilled alcohol. Infuse grappa or tequila with fruit or spices (see sidebar on page 93).

ACTIVITIES

Focus on games you can play at the table such as TableTopics, Who Am I?, Cards Against Humanity, and Two Truths and a Lie.

PARTY PROJECT

Buy floating paper lanterns. Have everyone write down wishes and place them in the lanterns. After dinner, light the lanterns and have a mass ascension.

KEEP THE PARTY GOING

Hire a magician or a musician, or screen an outdoor movie! You can buy a projector for under $100 and pair it to a smartphone or an iPad. Shine it on a blank wall, hook up some speakers, pop some popcorn—it's like you're at the drive-in!

SBAGLIATO COCKTAIL

This refreshing yet potent Negroni-inspired cocktail is pretty much all alcohol, so sip slowly! The mildly bitter Campari helps open up your appetite and enhance the flavor of other foods.

Ice

3 ounces Campari

3 ounces sweet vermouth

6 to 8 ounces prosecco

2 orange wheels, for garnish

1. Fill two white wine glasses halfway with ice and pour 1½ ounces each of the Campari and the vermouth into each one.

2. Stir at least twenty times (a colder drink will allow the prosecco to remain bubblier longer).

3. Add prosecco to fill the glasses three-quarters of the way.

4. Swipe an orange wheel around the rim of each glass, then drop it into the glass before serving.

MAKES 2 DRINKS

PREP TIME
5 minutes

ACTIVE TIME
5 minutes

TOTAL TIME
10 minutes

EASY

FIGS

WITH GOAT CHEESE AND PINK PEPPERCORN HONEY

¼ cup sliced almonds

½ cup honey

1 tablespoon whole pink peppercorns, lightly crushed

16 ripe fresh figs

4 ounces fresh goat's-milk cheese (chèvre)

Kosher salt

1. Preheat the oven to 350°F.

2. Spread the almonds on a small baking sheet and toast in the oven until lightly golden, 6 to 7 minutes; transfer to a plate and set aside to cool.

3. In a small saucepan, warm the honey and pink peppercorns over medium-low heat until the honey is warm and fluid but hasn't come to a simmer, 4 to 5 minutes. Remove from the heat and let the honey cool completely.

4. Cut off the top ½ inch of each fig. Use a very small spoon to scoop out the seeds from each fig, creating a hollowed-out core, and transfer the seeds to a small bowl. Add the goat cheese, 2 tablespoons of the cooled honey, and a pinch of salt to the seeds and stir to combine. Spoon the mixture into the figs with a small spoon. Drizzle the figs with the remaining honey and top with the toasted almonds before serving.

SERVES 16

PREP TIME
5 minutes

ACTIVE TIME
15 minutes

TOTAL TIME
30 minutes

MODERATE

So **simple**, so **satisfying**, so wow. If there's any cheese filling left over, it's fantastic spread on toast or crackers!

PORCINI-RUBBED RIB EYE STEAK

WITH OVEN-DRIED TOMATOES AND ARUGULA

FOR THE STEAKS

¼ cup broken-up small pieces of dried porcini mushrooms, or ¼ cup porcini mushroom powder (available from Amazon)

2 tablespoons kosher salt

2 tablespoons whole black peppercorns

1 tablespoon granulated garlic

1 tablespoon sugar

1 tablespoon red pepper flakes

3 (1-inch-thick) bone-in or boneless rib eye steaks

Olive oil, for the grill pan

FOR THE SALAD

3 cups baby arugula

Juice of 1 small lemon

Oven-Dried Tomatoes (recipe follows)

Balsamic vinegar reduction, for drizzling

SPECIAL EQUIPMENT

spice grinder or mortar and pestle, outdoor grill or grill pan

1. Make the steaks: If you're using whole dried porcinis and have a spice grinder, process the mushrooms in the spice grinder until they form a fine powder; transfer to a jar or small bowl. Process the salt and peppercorns in the same grinder and add them to the mushroom powder. Process the granulated garlic, sugar, and red pepper flakes in the grinder, add them to the spice mixture, and shake (or stir) to combine. (If you don't have a spice grinder, use the dried porcini powder and pound everything in a mortar and pestle.)

2. Place the spice mixture on a rimmed baking sheet and coat all sides of the steaks evenly with the spices.

3. Lightly coat a grill or grill pan with olive oil. Heat the grill to medium-high or heat the grill pan over medium-high heat. Place the steaks on the grill and cook until they feel like the flesh between your thumb and your pointer finger when lightly pressed, 4 to 5 minutes per side for bone-in and 3 to 4 minutes per side for boneless. Transfer to a cutting board and let rest while you make the salad.

4. Make the salad: In a medium bowl, toss the arugula with the lemon juice; transfer to a large platter.

5. Slice the steaks crosswise into ½-inch-thick pieces and against the grain, then arrange the steak over the salad. Sprinkle the oven-dried cherry tomatoes over the steak and drizzle with balsamic vinegar reduction before serving.

SERVES 3 TO 6

PREP TIME
10 minutes

ACTIVE TIME
25 minutes

TOTAL TIME
35 minutes

EASY

Since there's **sugar** in the rub, make sure to tend to your steaks so they don't **burn**. Allow the steaks to **rest** for 7 to 10 minutes before serving.

Oven-Dried Tomatoes

Makes about 1 cup ◆ *Prep time:* 5 minutes ◆ *Active time:* 5 minutes ◆
Total time: 1 hour 40 minutes ◆ *Easy*

1 pint cherry tomatoes,
halved

2 tablespoons olive oil

½ teaspoon kosher salt

1. Preheat the oven to 300°F.

2. Place the tomatoes in a bowl, drizzle them with the olive oil, and sprinkle with the salt. Spread them over a rimmed baking sheet in a single layer. Toss to coat. Roast, tossing once halfway through the cooking time, until they shrivel and caramelize, about 1 hour 30 minutes. Remove from the oven and serve warm or at room temperature. (These can be kept in an airtight container in the refrigerator covered in olive oil for up to 2 months.)

ORANGE AND BASIL MARINATED

GRILLED VEGETABLES

Herby basil and zesty orange play well together in this dish. Once ready, these can sit out all day, but make sure to let the zucchini and eggplant fully cook, then let all the vegetables cool completely before covering them to avoid steaming them under plastic wrap or foil.

4 medium oranges

1 cup canola oil, plus more for oiling the grill or grill pan

¼ cup red wine vinegar

4 garlic cloves, lightly smashed

¼ cup sliced fresh chives

¼ teaspoon red pepper flakes

Kosher salt and freshly ground black pepper

2 medium carrots, cut lengthwise into ⅛-inch-thick pieces

2 small Japanese eggplant (about 1 pound), cut lengthwise into ⅛-inch-thick slices

2 yellow summer squash (about 1 pound), cut lengthwise into ⅛-inch-thick slices

2 zucchini (about 12 ounces), cut lengthwise into ⅛-inch-thick slices

1 red bell pepper (about 8 ounces), halved, cored, and sliced into ¾-inch-thick strips

1 yellow bell pepper (about 8 ounces), halved, cored, and sliced into ¾-inch-thick strips

1. Zest and juice the orange (you should get ¾ to 1 cup orange juice). Set aside half the orange zest for garnish and put the remainder in an extra-large plastic storage container. Add the orange juice, canola oil, vinegar, garlic, chives, red pepper flakes, and 1 teaspoon each of kosher salt and black pepper and whisk to combine; set aside.

2. Bring a large saucepan of heavily salted water to a boil (the water should taste like the sea). Add the carrots and cook, stirring occasionally, until they are tender-crisp, 1½ to 2 minutes; depending on the size of your saucepan, this might have to be done in batches. Drain the carrots in a colander and set aside on a baking sheet or plate to cool completely.

3. Add the cooled carrots, eggplant, summer squash, zucchini, bell peppers, mushrooms, fennel, and onions to the marinade. Gently stir to combine, then cover and refrigerate for at least 1 hour and up to 4 hours.

4. Lightly coat the outdoor grill or grill pan with oil. Heat the grill to medium-high or heat a grill pan over medium-high heat.

5. Remove the vegetables from the marinade and set them on a baking sheet. Discard the marinade.

6. Once the grill is hot, add the vegetables in a single layer (you will probably need to cook them in batches) and cook until they are tender-crisp and deeply charred in spots, flipping them occasionally and removing them from the grill as they finish cooking, about 5 minutes for the zucchini and up to 10 minutes for the eggplant.

7. Transfer the grilled vegetables to a large serving platter. Sprinkle the reserved orange zest over the vegetables, and garnish with the basil leaves and a sprinkle of flaky salt before serving.

SERVES 8

PREP TIME
30 minutes

ACTIVE TIME
35 minutes

TOTAL TIME
2 hours
45 minutes
(includes marinating time)

EASY

2 portobello mushrooms, stemmed, caps sliced into ¾-inch-thick strips

1 small fennel bulb, halved, cored, and sliced into ¾-inch-thick strips

2 large red onions, halved and sliced into ¾-inch-thick slices

Handful of fresh basil leaves, thinly sliced, for garnish

Flaky salt, for sprinkling

SPECIAL EQUIPMENT
outdoor grill or grill pan

GRILLED BRANZINO

WITH LEMON, GARLIC, AND HERBS

4 whole branzino (about 1 pound each), scaled and gutted (ask your fishmonger to do this)

2 tablespoons olive oil, plus more for oiling the grill or grill pan

Kosher salt and freshly ground black pepper

3 lemons, 2 sliced into thin rounds and 1 sliced into wedges

4 garlic cloves, thinly sliced

1 bunch flat-leaf parsley

1 bunch chives

1 bunch thyme

SPECIAL EQUIPMENT
outdoor grill or grill pan, kitchen twine

1. Heat an outdoor grill to medium-high or heat a grill pan over medium-high heat.

2. Pat the fish dry with paper towels. Rub the cavity and the outside of each fish with the olive oil and season them liberally all over with salt and pepper. Stuff the cavity of each fish with the lemon rounds, garlic, parsley, chives, and thyme, dividing them equally among the fish.

3. Truss the fish with two pieces of kitchen twine so that the lemon, garlic, and herbs are held snugly within the cavity of each fish.

4. Lightly coat an outdoor grill or grill pan with olive oil. Grill the fish until lightly charred and just cooked through, about 7 minutes per side.

5. Transfer the fish to a large serving platter, cut away and discard the kitchen twine, and serve with lemon wedges.

SERVES 4

PREP TIME
20 minutes

ACTIVE TIME
35 minutes

TOTAL TIME
35 minutes

MODERATE

When buying whole fish, look for clear (not cloudy) eyes, red gills, and smooth (not slimy) skin.

1

Start with fish in front of you, head on the left, then remove the head and tail.

2

Remove a strip of skin from the bottom (belly) of the fish, then pull out the herbs and lemon.

3

Remove the pectoral and dorsal fins, then flip the fish to remove the second pectoral fin.

4

Turn the fish so its back (top) is facing you, then lift the top fillet away from the backbone.

HOW TO DEBONE A FISH

5

Lift up and remove the backbone. Remove any other small bones that were left behind.

6

Discard the carcass and finish the fillets with lemon, olive oil, and salt.

WATERMELON SALAD
WITH ROASTED TOMATO OIL

FOR THE ROASTED TOMATO OIL

1½ cups cherry tomatoes, halved

½ cup plus 2 tablespoons olive oil

½ teaspoon kosher salt

FOR THE SALAD

8 cups chopped seedless watermelon

2 softball-size jicamas, peeled and cut into long, thin matchsticks (about 4 cups)

12 sprigs mint, coarsely chopped

½ cup roasted pistachios, coarsely chopped

8 ounces feta cheese, cut into ½-inch dice

¾ cup thinly sliced red onion

6 tablespoons red wine vinegar

½ teaspoon kosher salt, plus more as needed

1. Make the roasted tomato oil: Preheat the oven to 300°F.

2. In a small bowl, toss the cherry tomatoes, 2 tablespoons of the olive oil, and the salt and spread them out in a single layer on a rimmed baking sheet. Roast for about 1 hour, until very soft and wrinkled. Remove from the oven and let the tomatoes cool slightly, then transfer them to a blender with the remaining ½ cup olive oil and puree until thick and emulsified, about 30 seconds.

3. Strain the tomato puree through a fine-mesh sieve into a bowl, pressing down on the mixture to extract as much oil as possible (you should have about ½ cup roasted tomato oil). If you're not using it immediately, the oil can be stored in an airtight container in the refrigerator for up to 1 week.

4. Make the salad: In a large bowl, gently toss the watermelon, jicama, mint, pistachios, feta, and red onion to combine, then arrange on a large serving platter.

5. In a small bowl, whisk together ½ cup of the roasted tomato oil, the vinegar, and the salt. Drizzle the dressing over the watermelon salad before serving.

SERVES 12

PREP TIME
20 minutes

ACTIVE TIME
10 minutes

TOTAL TIME
1 hour 30 minutes

MODERATE

Slice your onions last to keep their flavor separate from that of the sweet, juicy watermelon.

MIXED BERRY TART

The first time I went to Ina Garten's house in the Hamptons, I made this tart for her, and I think it solidified our friendship. There are no rules, so if you prefer blackberries or strawberries, by all means, use them!

1 cup (2 sticks) unsalted butter

½ cup plus ⅓ cup granulated sugar

1¼ cups all-purpose flour

1 teaspoon kosher salt

½ teaspoon vanilla extract

2 large eggs

1 vanilla bean, split lengthwise and seeds scraped out, pod discarded or reserved for another use (see box on page 250)

2 (6-ounce) packages raspberries (3 cups)

1 (6-ounce) package blackberries (1½ cups)

Confectioners' sugar, for dusting (optional)

SPECIAL EQUIPMENT
9-inch tart pan with removable bottom

1. Preheat the oven to 375°F.

2. In a small saucepan, melt the butter over medium heat, then cook, stirring frequently, until deep golden brown but not burned, about 5 minutes. Remove from the heat and set aside.

3. In a medium bowl, combine ⅓ cup of the sugar, 1 cup of the flour, and the salt. Add ½ cup of the browned butter and the vanilla extract, then mix with your fingers until the mixture is crumbly and homogeneous, about 6 minutes.

4. Press the mixture into an even layer over the bottom and up the sides of a 9-inch tart pan with a removable bottom.

5. Use a fork to poke eight or nine holes all over the bottom of the tart shell and bake for 8 minutes, then rotate the pan 180 degrees and bake for 8 minutes more, until lightly golden. Remove the tart crust from the oven and let cool.

6. In a large bowl, whisk together the eggs, vanilla bean seeds, and the remaining ½ cup sugar until combined, then whisk in the remaining browned butter and the remaining ¼ cup flour; set aside. It should look thin and drippy.

7. Arrange the raspberries and blackberries in the tart pan, pointy-side up, starting with one ring of blackberries along the outside edge, then filling in with smaller and smaller rings of raspberries and ending with a small cluster of blackberries in the center.

8. Carefully pour the custard over the berries, filling in the spaces between them as best you can. Tap the tart pan on the counter so the filling oozes between the berries. Return the tart to the oven and bake, rotating the pan halfway through the cooking time, until the filling has risen, the top is golden brown, and a toothpick inserted into the center of the tart comes out dry (not including berry juice!), 35 to 40 minutes. Remove from the oven and let cool for 10 minutes, then sprinkle with confectioners' sugar, if desired. Slice and serve while still slightly warm or at room temperature.

SERVES 12

PREP TIME
20 minutes

ACTIVE TIME
20 minutes

TOTAL TIME
1 hour 20 minutes

EASY

SUMMER SOULstice

Come together now! Chances are you've been lending a hand to good causes in your community for as long as you can remember. But beyond the spaghetti dinners and PTA parties, why not throw an extra-special gathering to raise money for your favorite charity? Love pets? Make your organization the ASPCA. Into the environment? Create a fund-raiser to benefit your favorite earthbound mission. You don't need any restraints to be a do-gooder: Most places will even donate space if you are raising money for charity.

WHAT GUESTS CAN BRING
A dish to pass, appetizers, a willingness to help out, and their checkbooks!

PARTY BASICS

Ample seating area and shade for a large crowd. Large coolers filled with hydrating drinks. Colorful pledge cards guests can use to make donations and write personal messages to be passed on to the organization.

PARTY UPGRADES

A photo booth where guests can take pictures labeled with a special hashtag created to draw attention to the charity of choice.

OVER-THE-TOP IDEAS

Call in every favor you have to get a local celebrity to perform a set for charity. Set up an auction with donated items (designer clothing, vacations, meals at local restaurants) described and priced; hire an auctioneer to give the proceedings a professional flair.

GET GUESTS INVOLVED
Have guests volunteer as much as you can; they are there to help! Have them cook, ice down the sangria, do research on the organization in advance, and print out information about the event. Designate a few people who can welcome other guests with a hug and an explanation of the organization's mission.

WHAT TO WEAR
Clothes featuring the logo of the organization you are helping. T-shirts emblazoned with portraits of inspirational figures you admire (Gandhi, Martin Luther King Jr., Rosa Parks).

THE TABLE
Decorate your surfaces with cheery yellow gingham and accessories with wood tones: cups, plates, platters, and servingware in real wood or disposable bamboo.

THE FLOWERS
Yellow flowers like chrysanthemums, which represent loyalty and love; and daisies, which symbolize innocence and purity.

THE DRINKS
Plenty of water, soul-stirring iced tea made with warm spices like cinnamon sticks and star anise; a wine that donates a portion of its profits to a favorite charity.

PLAN AHEAD
- *Three Days Before:* Bake the cake and make the pesto.
- *Two Days Before:* Assemble the cake; shuck the corn.
- *One Day Before:* Marinate the chicken, chop the herbs, and cut the lemons.

HOST CRAFT PROJECT
Since this is a group effort, have the craft project be participatory as well. Designate a wall with butcher paper, poster board, and your charity's logo on it, and have everyone write a wish for what they hope the future will bring for the charity.

ACTIVITIES
Set up a telethon phone bank: Arrange a table where guests can sit and use their cell phones to raise money for the cause. Send an email thank-you note that all the fund-raisers can use to follow up with their pledges and send links for where to make an actual donation.

PARTY PROJECT
Allow guests to craft their own flower wreaths with flexible wire, gardening tape, and an abundance of fresh flowers you've brought in for the occasion.

GIFTS FOR GUESTS
Send guests home with piggy banks decorated to identify a favorite charity. Ask them to fill the piggy banks and send the proceeds along. Many sponsors will supply products you can send home with people in cool swag bags.

KEEP THE PARTY GOING
Bring in an inspirational preacher or speaker (or a gospel choir!) to rouse the crowd, then pass a plate around, revival-style, to ask for one more round of generosity.

This is a **home-run dessert**. Make the cake Neapolitan—with chocolate, vanilla, and strawberry to choose from, everyone is happy!

PLAYLIST

"Ain't No Mountain High Enough," Marvin Gaye and Tammi Terrell

"I'm Still Standing," Elton John

"Born This Way," Lady Gaga

"Born to Run," Bruce Springsteen

"Don't Stop Believin'," Journey

"I'm Alive," Céline Dion

"Man in the Mirror," Michael Jackson

"One Moment in Time," Whitney Houston

"Same Love," Macklemore and Ryan Lewis

"Stronger (What Doesn't Kill You)," Kelly Clarkson

"True Colors," Cyndi Lauper

"We Are the World," USA for Africa

SANGRIA

Canola oil

½ cup plus 2 tablespoons sugar

2 medium peaches, halved, pits removed but reserved

2 or 3 ripe red plums, halved, pits removed but reserved

½ cup water

½ lemon, scrubbed and sliced into thin rounds

½ medium orange, scrubbed and sliced into thin rounds

2 cups peach nectar

⅓ cup brandy

1 (750-milliliter) bottle rosé wine

Ice

SPECIAL EQUIPMENT
outdoor grill or grill pan

1. Very lightly coat an outdoor grill or grill pan with the oil. Heat the grill to medium-high or heat a grill pan over medium-high heat.

2. Sprinkle 2 tablespoons of the sugar evenly over the cut sides of the peaches and plums. Grill the fruit cut-side down until deep char marks appear and the fruit easily releases from the grill, about 2 minutes. Transfer to a cutting board and let cool completely.

3. In a medium saucepan, combine the remaining ½ cup sugar, the reserved fruit pits, and the water. Bring to a simmer over medium heat and cook, stirring, until the sugar has completely dissolved, about 3 minutes. Remove from the heat and let cool to room temperature, then strain the syrup through a fine-mesh sieve into a large pitcher and discard the pits.

4. Cut the grilled fruit into ¼-inch-thick slices and add them to the pitcher along with the lemon rounds, orange rounds, peach nectar, brandy, and wine. Stir to combine, then cover with plastic wrap and refrigerate until the flavors have melded and the fruit takes on the flavor of the sangria, at least 6 hours and up to overnight.

5. Serve over ice in your glass of choice, adding a few pieces of fruit from the pitcher for garnish.

MAKES 14 DRINKS

PREP TIME
15 minutes

ACTIVE TIME
10 minutes

TOTAL TIME
6 hours
25 minutes
(includes chilling time)

EASY

VIRGIN CHARRED PEACH AND PLUM
SANGRIA

Replace the brandy and wine with 2 cups chilled brewed black tea.

◆

No need to leave the fruit on the grill too long; just a couple of minutes gives you that **perfect touch of smoke**.

RICE PILAF

WITH TOASTED ALMONDS

5 cups low-sodium chicken stock

Kosher salt

6 tablespoons (¾ stick) unsalted butter

1 small yellow onion, finely diced (1 cup)

1 garlic clove, minced

1 cup broken capellini pasta (roughly ¾-inch-long pieces)

2 cups long-grain white rice, well rinsed and drained

½ cup sliced almonds

1. Preheat the oven to 375°F.

2. In a medium saucepan, combine the stock and a large pinch of salt and bring to a simmer over medium heat; cover and keep warm (reduce the heat if it starts to boil).

3. Heat a dry 10-inch skillet over medium-high heat. Add the butter and swirl it in the pan until melted, then add the onion, a pinch of salt, and a splash of water; cook, stirring occasionally, until the onion is softened and lightly golden, 3 to 4 minutes. Add the garlic and cook for 2 minutes more. Add the pasta and cook, stirring, until toasted, 2 to 3 minutes. Stir in the rice and cook until lightly toasted, 2 to 3 minutes.

4. Carefully pour the hot stock into the rice mixture and bring to a boil, then reduce the heat to maintain a very low simmer, cover with a tight-fitting lid, and cook until the rice and pasta are tender and all the liquid has been absorbed, 10 to 11 minutes. Turn off the heat and let the rice sit, covered, for 5 minutes.

5. While the rice is cooking, spread the almonds over a small baking sheet and toast in the oven until lightly browned, 8 to 9 minutes. Transfer to a plate to cool.

6. Fluff the rice with a fork, taste, and season with salt. Stir in all but 2 tablespoons of the almonds. Transfer to a serving dish and garnish with the reserved almonds.

SERVES 6 TO 8

PREP TIME
5 minutes

ACTIVE TIME
35 minutes

TOTAL TIME
35 minutes

MEDITERRANEAN CHICKEN

1 tablespoon dried oregano

2 dried bay leaves, broken in half

3 garlic cloves, minced

½ cup olive oil

¼ cup red wine vinegar

1 (6¾-ounce) jar pimiento-stuffed Spanish olives, drained

1 (3½-ounce) jar capers in brine, drained

4 ounces dried cranberries (1 cup)

4 ounces dried apricots (1 cup), torn in half

6 ounces dried pitted prunes (1 heaping cup)

1 teaspoon kosher salt

1 teaspoon freshly ground black pepper

8 boneless, skinless chicken breasts (about 4 pounds total), patted dry

1 cup lightly packed light brown sugar

¼ cup dry white wine

2 tablespoons coarsely chopped fresh flat-leaf parsley, for garnish

When I first arrived in LA, I worked as a waiter for Tom Peters, an art-world caterer. He taught me to make this dish, inspired by the legendary chicken marbella in *The Silver Palate Cookbook*. He showed me how to throw the chicken in Tupperware to marinate, then roast it in a baking dish. It always got rave reviews! It's flavorful, simple, and a favorite of mine to this day.

1. In a large plastic storage container with a lid, stir together the oregano, bay leaves, garlic, olive oil, vinegar, olives, capers, cranberries, apricots, prunes, salt, and pepper. Add the chicken, then use clean hands to gently coat the chicken in the marinade. Cover and refrigerate for 12 to 24 hours.

2. Remove the chicken from the refrigerator and let it rest at room temperature for 30 minutes.

3. Preheat the oven to 350°F.

4. Using your hands, transfer the chicken to a large skillet or 9 by 13-inch baking dish, tucking under the sides of each chicken breast so it looks like a ball. Spoon the fruit and any remaining marinade into the pan.

5. Sprinkle the brown sugar evenly over the chicken pieces, then drizzle with the wine. Bake until the juices run clear and the skin on the chicken is lightly browned, about 1 hour, rotating the pan from front to back halfway through the cooking time.

6. Transfer the chicken to a serving platter and spoon the fruit and liquid from the pan over the chicken (discard the bay leaves). Garnish with the parsley before serving alongside the Rice Pilaf (page 117).

SERVES 8

PREP TIME
10 minutes

ACTIVE TIME
1 hour 10 minutes

TOTAL TIME
25 hours
10 minutes
(includes marinating time)

EASY

LEMON SOLE

FOR A BIG GROUP

4 pounds lemon sole fillets

1¼ cups (2½ sticks) unsalted butter

2 shallots, thinly sliced (about ½ cup)

1 tablespoon kosher salt

1 (2-ounce) jar capers, drained and coarsely chopped (about ½ cup)

Leaves from ½ bunch flat-leaf parsley, finely chopped (about ½ cup), plus a few sprigs for garnish

Grated zest and juice of 2 lemons, plus 1 lemon, thinly sliced

SPECIAL EQUIPMENT
fish spatula

1. Preheat the oven to 400°F. Place two rimmed baking sheets on two racks in the oven and allow to preheat for 10 minutes.

2. Pat the fish dry with paper towels. Cut ½ cup (1 stick) of the butter into cubes. Once the baking sheets are heated, take them out of the oven and distribute half the butter cubes over them. Scatter half the sliced shallots over the baking sheets and arrange the sole on top of the butter and shallots, making sure the fillets don't overlap. Top the fillets with the remaining butter cubes and shallot slices, then sprinkle ½ teaspoon of the salt evenly over each baking sheet. Return the sheets to the oven and bake until the fish is mostly opaque but still firm, 8 to 10 minutes.

3. Meanwhile, in a small saucepan, melt the remaining ¾ cup (1½ sticks) butter over medium-low heat. Remove from the heat and pour into a medium heatproof bowl. Add the capers, parsley, lemon zest, lemon juice, and the remaining 2 teaspoons salt and stir to combine.

4. Remove the baking sheets from the oven. Using a fish spatula, transfer the fillets to a serving platter. Transfer the shallots as well, but discard the liquid left behind in the pan. Pour the caper sauce over the fillets and garnish with parsley sprigs and lemon slices before serving.

SERVES 18

PREP TIME
15 minutes

ACTIVE TIME
10 minutes

TOTAL TIME
30 minutes

EASY

◆

You can come home from work and have this **gourmet dinner in minutes**; think minimum effort, maximum impact!

WHOLE

ROASTED CORN

Grilling this corn in the husks steams it perfectly. If you have leftover corn, make a free-form corn salad.

12 ears sweet corn, husks on

1 cup mayonnaise

1 tablespoon kosher salt

1 teaspoon freshly ground black pepper

6 limes

1 cup freshly grated Pecorino Romano cheese (1½ ounces)

½ teaspoon red pepper flakes, plus more to taste

SPECIAL EQUIPMENT
outdoor grill or grill pan

1. Heat an outdoor grill to medium-high or heat a grill pan over medium-high heat (or set a rack in the center of the oven and preheat the broiler).

2. Carefully peel back the corn husks, leaving them attached at the base, and remove and discard the silks (the white threads between the corn and the husks). Set aside.

3. In a small bowl, combine the mayonnaise, salt, and pepper.

4. Using an offset spatula, butter knife, or your hands, rub each ear of corn with a heaping tablespoon of the seasoned mayonnaise, then carefully fold the corn husks back over the kernels, twisting gently at the tip of each ear to seal.

5. Grill the corn, rotating the ears every 5 minutes or so, until the husks are mostly black and the kernels have started to char a bit, 25 minutes total. (If you're broiling the corn, set the ears on a wire rack set over a large baking sheet and broil, rotating them as directed.) When the corn is nearly done, quarter the limes lengthwise and grill or broil them until lightly charred, about 5 minutes.

6. Remove the corn and limes from the grill and let cool slightly. Remove and discard the corn husks (don't worry if a few charred bits of husk remain attached to the corn—that gives it flavor).

7. Spread the cheese out on a small baking dish or plate. Squeeze a grilled lime wedge over each ear of corn, then roll the corn in the cheese to coat. Arrange the corn on a large platter, sprinkle with red pepper flakes, and serve with the extra lime wedges on the side.

SERVES 12

PREP TIME
5 minutes

ACTIVE TIME
30 minutes

TOTAL TIME
40 minutes

EASY

PASTA

This delicious mint pesto pasta freezes well, so if you're not throwing a big party, freeze the pesto in ice cube trays until solid, then pop them into a container or zip-top bag and store for pesto whenever you want it!

Kosher salt and freshly ground black pepper

1 (1-pound) box bow-tie pasta (farfalle)

4 cups packed fresh mint leaves (about 4 ounces), plus several whole leaves for garnish

1 garlic clove, lightly crushed

3 tablespoons unsalted roasted pistachios (see Note)

1 cup extra-virgin olive oil

1 (2½-ounce) wedge Parmesan cheese

Juice of ½ large lemon

Dollop of unsalted butter (optional)

1. Bring a large pot of heavily salted water to a boil (the water should taste like the sea). Cook the pasta according to the package instructions until al dente.

2. While the pasta is cooking, in a food processor, combine the mint leaves, garlic, and pistachios and pulse until finely chopped, about 10 pulses. While still pulsing, slowly drizzle in the olive oil, then remove the lid and use your hands to break the Parmesan into small chunks, dropping them into the food processor. Season with a pinch each of salt and pepper. Pulse until the pesto is well combined but there are still small pieces of Parmesan visible throughout the mixture, being careful not to overblend (or the mint will turn black), about 5 pulses.

3. Taste the pesto and season with salt and pepper. Transfer the pesto to a large, high-sided skillet. Use a large slotted spoon to lift the pasta out of the pot directly onto the pesto; toss to combine and turn the heat to medium-high. Cook, stirring occasionally, until any excess water from the pasta has evaporated and some of the Parmesan has started to melt, 3 to 4 minutes.

4. Stir in the lemon juice and butter (if using). Taste and season with salt and pepper. Transfer to a large platter and garnish with additional mint leaves. Serve warm or at room temperature.

Note *To roast your own pistachios, spread them in an even layer over a rimmed baking sheet and roast in a preheated 350°F oven for 8 to 9 minutes. Remove from the oven and transfer to a plate to cool before adding to the food processor.*

SERVES 10

PREP TIME
10 minutes

ACTIVE TIME
25 minutes

TOTAL TIME
25 minutes

EASY

NEAPOLITAN ICE CREAM SANDWICH CAKE

This sandwich may require some extra effort, but the visual presentation of one whole ice cream cake, ready to be sliced and enjoyed by kids of all ages, makes it worth it. Besides—now you'll have a lock-and-load dessert for weeks!

¼ cup canola oil, or as needed

¾ cup boiling water

¾ cup unsweetened Dutch-process cocoa powder

½ cup bittersweet chocolate chips

1 cup buttermilk

2 cups all-purpose flour

2 teaspoons baking soda

1 teaspoon kosher salt

½ cup plus 6 tablespoons (1¾ sticks) unsalted butter

1½ cups packed light brown sugar

1 teaspoon vanilla extract

3 large eggs

3 (1½-quart) tubs of ice cream— one each of chocolate, vanilla, and strawberry

SPECIAL EQUIPMENT
large straw

1. Preheat the oven to 350°F. Grease a 13 by 18-inch rimmed baking sheet with canola oil, line with parchment paper, then grease the top of the parchment with more oil.

2. In a large bowl, combine the boiling water and cocoa powder and whisk until smooth, then add the chocolate chips and stir until melted and smooth. Stir in the buttermilk.

3. In a small bowl, whisk together the flour, baking soda, and salt and set aside.

4. In the bowl of a stand mixer fitted with the paddle attachment, beat the butter and brown sugar until light and fluffy, about 2 minutes. Add the vanilla, then add the eggs one at a time and beat until combined, scraping down the sides of the bowl with a rubber spatula as needed.

5. Reduce the mixer speed to low and add the chocolate mixture all at once. Beat until incorporated, then add the dry ingredients in three additions, beating until just combined after each and scraping down the sides of the bowl as needed.

6. Pour the batter into the prepared pan. Bake until the cake is no longer jiggly and a toothpick inserted into the center comes out clean, about 20 minutes, rotating the pan halfway through the cooking time. Remove from the oven and let the cake cool completely in the pan.

7. Invert the cooled cake onto a cutting board and remove the parchment paper. Cut off 1¼ inches from the two short ends of the cake, then cut the cake in half lengthwise. You should now have two cake pieces, roughly 6 by 13½ inches each.

8. Line another baking sheet with parchment paper, invert the two cakes onto it, and freeze for at least 30 minutes or overnight.

SERVES 20

PREP TIME
20 minutes

ACTIVE TIME
20 minutes

TOTAL TIME
2 hours
30 minutes
(includes cooling and freezing time)

INVOLVED

9. Transfer one piece of the chilled cake to a large plate; this will be the bottom of your "ice cream sandwich." This is where you need to work fast and be precise. Cut open the ice cream cartons and discard the packaging. If necessary, square off the edges of the blocks of ice cream into rectangles. Place all three blocks of ice cream in a row directly on the cake layer on the platter, so that they lie flush with one another. Cover the platter with plastic wrap, put it back in the freezer, and freeze for at least 30 minutes or overnight.

10. Meanwhile, use a large plastic straw (a large smoothie straw is best) to carefully make three rows of holes down the length of the remaining cake layer so it resembles the top of an ice cream sandwich. Remove the platter from the freezer and top the ice cream with the perforated cake layer. Freeze, covered, until ready to serve.

SUNDAY FUNDAY

Embrace the sheer fun of summer by celebrating its essential basics: grilling, good friends, and awesome weather. A backyard, a rooftop, or a community center all make perfect spots to throw a rollicking outdoor party.

PARTY BASICS

Yard games like a potato sack race, watermelon seed spitting contest, water balloon toss, duck duck goose, tug-of-war, and jump rope.

PARTY UPGRADES

Fill a kiddie pool with VERY soapy water (use dish soap!) and make a huge bubble area complete with Hula-hoops, two giant strings on a stick, and bubble wands. Make your own photo booth by hanging an oversize frame on a tree from both ends. String beach balls together to make a fun garland. Play games like ring around a lawn flamingo. Organize a water balloon toss.

OVER-THE-TOP IDEAS

Set up a cozy tent with pillows and blankets underneath for a break from the sun, or hang gauzy curtains to achieve both a whimsical look and some much-needed shade. Make an over-the-top s'mores area with a line of sternos—use marshmallows, graham crackers, and your favorite full-size candy bars.

WHAT GUESTS CAN BRING
Outdoor games, fireworks, sparklers, water toys, watermelon slices and cut-up fruit, chips, dips, drinks, and plenty of ice.

GET GUESTS INVOLVED
Ask guests to help set up games and a tie-dye station, make the slushies, and pass the tofu skewers as an appetizer. It can get lonely all by yourself at the grill, so find someone to hang with you while you are grilling and hold the platter for the finished food.

WHAT TO WEAR
Light and easy clothes, tank tops, Daisy Duke cutoffs, swimsuits, shorts, sundresses, and sunscreen.

THE TABLE
Dress up any outside picnic table with a brightly colored cloth. Use yellow, orange, or blue runner fabric with thick stripes. Use sand toys as vases for flowers.

THE FLOWERS
Brightly colored blooms, or sunflowers in all different hues. Gloriosa daisies and coreopsis.

THE DRINKS
Plenty of water, sodas, and juices. Fill a Radio Flyer wagon with ice and nestle your drinks inside.

PLAN AHEAD
- *Three Days Before:* Freeze ice cubes for the mojitos; make your peanut sauce.
- *Two Days Before:* Make the barbecue sauce, vinaigrette, and all of the ice cream sauces.
- *One Day Before:* Brine the ribs and marinate the tofu; assemble the sundae bar; pre-scoop ice cream.

HOST CRAFT PROJECT
When people arrive, hand out a welcome gift consisting of a small sand bucket filled with sunscreen, mineral water mist spray, cheap sunglasses, and lip balm.

ACTIVITIES
Tag, Frisbee, monkey in the middle, red light green light, red rover, scavenger hunts, ladder golf, corn hole, What time is it, Mr. Fox?, horseshoes, bocce ball, kick the can, capture the flag, badminton, croquet, Slip'N Slide, limbo, paddle board, or pool games like Marco Polo and world's craziest dive.

PARTY PROJECT
Tie-dye! Set up a tie-dyeing station; consult online resources beforehand for helpful tips. Provide a rainbow of dyes, rubber bands, and instructions printed out on tie-dye stationery you can order in advance online. Before the party, tell people to bring a favorite white piece of clothing for their custom-dyed garment.

GIFTS FOR GUESTS
Goodie bags for the kids—sand buckets filled with sidewalk chalk, squirt guns, cheap sunglasses, Kool-Aid, bubbles, sparklers, freezer pops, candy, Frisbees, balloons, and glow sticks. For the adults, fill buckets with sunscreen, moisturizer, beach towels, water bottles, and mani-pedi kits.

KEEP THE PARTY GOING
Host an all-night disco dance party with props and a disco ball hung from a tree.

PLAYLIST

"California Soul," Marlena Shaw

"Too Hot," Prince Buster

"Summertime Blues,"
Eddie Cochran

"Summer," Calvin Harris

"Summer of '69," Bryan Adams

"Summer Girls," LFO

"Cruel Summer," Bananarama

"The Boys of Summer,"
Don Henley

**"Those Lazy-Hazy-Crazy Days of
Summer,"** Nat King Cole

"Summertime," Magnetic North
and Taiyo Na

"Summer in the City,"
The Lovin' Spoonful

"Darlin'," The Beach Boys

"Cool for the Summer,"
Demi Lovato

MOJITO SLUSHIES

2 cups fresh lime juice (from 12 to 16 limes)

2 cups Fresh Mint Simple Syrup (see page 78)

½ cup water

Ice

24 ounces white rum (or 24 ounces lemonade for a mocktail)

Mint sprigs, for garnish

1. In a pitcher or large glass liquid measuring cup, thoroughly mix the lime juice, simple syrup, and water. Pour the mixture into ice cube trays and freeze completely, at least 6 hours.

2. To make a batch of 6 mojito slushies, count out half the frozen mint-lime cubes and put them in a blender. Add about two-thirds the amount of regular ice cubes as mint-lime cubes, then pour in 12 ounces of the rum or lemonade and blend until smooth.

3. Divide the slushies among six glasses and garnish each with a mint sprig before serving. Blend the second batch of slushies just before serving them so they don't melt!

MAKES 12 DRINKS
(2 batches of 6)

PREP TIME
40 minutes

ACTIVE TIME
15 minutes

TOTAL TIME
6 hours (*includes freezing time*)

EASY

These easy, amazing drinks are **stealthily alcoholic**, so be careful!

GRILLED POTATO AND LEEK SALAD

WITH SALSA VERDE VINAIGRETTE

FOR THE POTATOES AND LEEKS

Kosher salt

3 pounds fingerling potatoes

1 tablespoon whole black peppercorns

3 large leeks (about 1½ pounds)

¼ cup plus 3 tablespoons olive oil

FOR THE SALSA VERDE VINAIGRETTE

¼ cup whole-grain mustard

¼ cup white wine vinegar

½ cup extra-virgin olive oil

1½ teaspoons kosher salt, plus more for seasoning

4 scallions, thinly sliced

Leaves from 1 large bunch flat-leaf parsley, finely chopped

1 bunch cilantro

¼ cup sliced radishes, for garnish

SPECIAL EQUIPMENT

outdoor grill or grill pan

1. Cook the potatoes: Bring a large stockpot of heavily salted water to a boil (the water should taste like the sea). Add the potatoes and peppercorns, reduce the heat to medium-low, and simmer the potatoes until tender, about 20 minutes.

2. While the potatoes are cooking, make the salsa verde vinaigrette: In a medium bowl, whisk together the mustard, vinegar, olive oil, and salt. Stir in the scallions, parsley, and cilantro.

3. Grill the leeks: Heat the grill or grill pan to medium-high.

4. Slice off the root ends and dark green tops of the leeks and discard. Halve the leeks lengthwise, then peel back the layers by the base so they are slightly separated. Immerse the leeks in a bowl of cold water and gently shake to dislodge any dirt and grit. Pat dry, then drizzle with 3 tablespoons of the olive oil and sprinkle liberally with salt. Grill the leeks cut-side down until dark grill marks form, about 4 minutes, then flip and cook until the leeks no longer feel stiff, about 4 minutes more. Transfer to a plate and let cool.

5. When the potatoes are tender, drain them and spread them out on a baking sheet to cool, discarding the peppercorns. Once cool enough to touch, slice them in half lengthwise and toss with the remaining ¼ cup olive oil and 2 teaspoons salt. Grill, cut-side down, until dark grill marks appear, 3 to 4 minutes, then flip and grill for 3 minutes more.

6. Toss the potatoes, leeks, and salsa verde vinaigrette in a large bowl; garnish with the radishes. The salad can be served right away or allowed to sit on the counter for 2 to 3 hours before serving.

SERVES 6 TO 8

PREP TIME
15 minutes

ACTIVE TIME
15 minutes

TOTAL TIME
45 minutes

MODERATE

The **charred leeks** really make this salad special. I wouldn't substitute anything else for those, but use **any kind of potatoes** you like.

GRILLED TOFU SKEWERS

WITH COCONUT-PEANUT DIPPING SAUCE

The crispy outside and gooey center make these skewers a vegan dream come true! Take the extra time to really press out as much water as possible; it allows the tofu to take on maximum flavor. And mop that grill generously with olive oil so the tofu doesn't stick.

FOR THE COCONUT-PEANUT DIPPING AND GRILLING SAUCE

1 (13.5-ounce) can full-fat, unsweetened coconut milk

1 garlic clove, finely grated on a Microplane

1 (2-inch) piece fresh ginger, peeled and grated on a Microplane

3 tablespoons soy sauce

6 tablespoons smooth natural peanut butter

Juice of 1 lime (2 tablespoons), plus more to taste

FOR THE GRILLED TOFU

2 (14-ounce) packages extra-firm tofu (not silken)

Vegetable oil, for grilling

SPECIAL EQUIPMENT

6-inch wooden skewers, preferably the flat kind, soaked in water for 30 minutes; outdoor grill or grill pan

1. Make the sauce: In a food processor, combine the coconut milk, garlic, ginger, soy sauce, peanut butter, and lime juice and process until smooth, about 1 minute.

2. Make the grilled tofu: Drain the tofu, then cut each block widthwise into 6 even slices. Stack a few sheets of heavy-duty paper towels or clean kitchen towels on a clean work surface, place the tofu slices in a single layer on top of the towels, and gently press on the slices to remove excess moisture. Repeat once more with fresh towels until the tofu is fairly dry (this step helps the tofu become extra crisp!).

3. Arrange the tofu in a shallow baking dish and coat with half the sauce. Cover and refrigerate for at least 1 hour and up to overnight.

4. Transfer the remaining sauce to a small saucepan and cook over medium heat, stirring frequently, until the sauce thickens slightly and darkens a bit in color, 10 to 11 minutes. Remove from the heat and let cool.

5. Heat an outdoor grill to medium-high or heat a grill pan over medium-high heat. Once hot, scrape down the grates with a grill brush and use a rag and a set of tongs to carefully coat the grates with a generous amount of vegetable oil. Coat the grates a second time with oil, then carefully place the tofu slices on the grill and grill until the tofu develops deep grill marks and is lightly charred and crispy, about 12 minutes, then flip and grill for 4 minutes more.

6. Remove the tofu slices, let cool slightly, then cut each piece in half widthwise and insert a wooden skewer lengthwise, about three-quarters of the way through the tofu. Arrange the skewers on a platter and serve with the peanut dipping sauce on the side.

SERVES 4

PREP TIME
10 minutes

ACTIVE TIME
45 minutes

TOTAL TIME
1 hour 20 minutes
(includes marinating time)

EASY

GRILLED RIBS

WITH COLA BARBECUE SAUCE

FOR THE BRINE

5 quarts cold water

3/4 cup kosher salt

1 cup packed dark brown sugar

2 large yellow onions (1½ pounds),
halved and sliced

2 tablespoons whole black
peppercorns, lightly smashed

2 tablespoons yellow mustard seeds,
lightly smashed

2 dried bay leaves, torn in half

1 large bunch thyme

3 racks baby back ribs (about
7½ pounds total), each rack halved

FOR THE SPICE RUB

1 tablespoon coriander seeds

1 tablespoon cumin seeds

3/4 teaspoon whole black peppercorns

3/4 teaspoon ancho chile powder

1 tablespoon kosher salt

1 tablespoon dry mustard

1 tablespoon granulated garlic

1½ tablespoons smoked paprika

3 tablespoons packed dark brown sugar

FOR THE COLA BARBECUE SAUCE

4 cups cola

1 vanilla bean, split lengthwise and
seeds scraped out; or 1 tablespoon
vanilla paste

1 tablespoon canola oil

1 small onion (4 ounces), coarsely
chopped

Kosher salt

1½ cups ketchup

1. Make the brine: In a large stockpot (at least 10 quarts—large enough to hold both the brine and the ribs), stir together the water, salt, brown sugar, onions, peppercorns, mustard seeds, bay leaves, and thyme. Bring to a boil over high heat, stirring occasionally, until the salt and sugar have just dissolved, about 10 minutes. Remove from the heat and let cool completely, about 2 hours.

2. Add the ribs to the brine, cover with a lid or plastic wrap, and refrigerate for at least 6 hours and up to 24 hours.

3. Make the spice rub: In a spice grinder or mortar and pestle, grind the coriander seeds, cumin seeds, and peppercorns until finely ground. Transfer the spices to a medium bowl and add the ancho chile powder, salt, dry mustard, granulated garlic, paprika, and brown sugar. Whisk to combine.

4. Make the cola barbecue sauce: In a medium saucepan, combine the cola and the vanilla bean seeds and pod and bring to a boil. Cook until the mixture has reduced to 1 cup, 35 to 40 minutes. Pour the reduced cola into a medium bowl and let cool slightly.

5. Rinse out the saucepan, then return it to the stovetop over medium heat. Add the canola oil, swirl to coat the pan, then add the onion, a pinch of salt, and a splash of water and cook, stirring occasionally, until the onion has softened, 8 to 9 minutes. Stir in the reduced cola, ketchup, vinegar, Worcestershire, liquid smoke, and 2 tablespoons of the spice rub. Bring to a boil, then reduce the heat to maintain a simmer and cook until slightly thickened, 10 to 12 minutes.

6. Use an immersion blender to carefully blend the sauce directly in the pot until smooth. (Alternatively, carefully transfer the sauce to a regular blender and blend until smooth.) Taste and season with salt. Pour the sauce into a medium bowl and let cool completely. Cover with plastic wrap and refrigerate alongside the ribs.

7. Cook the ribs: One hour before you plan to cook the ribs, remove them from the brine, place them on a large baking sheet, and pat them dry with paper towels.

SERVES 6 TO 8

PREP TIME
20 minutes

ACTIVE TIME
2 hours 10 minutes

TOTAL TIME
8 hours
30 minutes
(includes minimum brining time)

INVOLVED

I once fed these
to my **kids**, who
don't drink soda,
close to bedtime,
and they were
**bouncing off
the walls**!

2 tablespoons apple cider vinegar

2 teaspoons Worcestershire sauce

1 teaspoon liquid smoke

Canola oil, for cooking

Thyme sprigs, for serving

SPECIAL EQUIPMENT
outdoor grill or grill pan; spice grinder or mortar and pestle

8. Lightly oil your grill or grill pan (I usually use an old, clean towel to season the grill with canola oil). Heat the grill or a grill pan to medium-high heat.

9. Transfer half the barbecue sauce to a separate bowl and set it aside for serving alongside the ribs.

10. Using your hands, distribute the spice rub all over the ribs, evenly coating the top and bottom of the meat.

11. Place the ribs on the grill and sear until they are crispy and have distinct grill marks, about 5 minutes per side. Reduce the heat to low, basting the ribs with half the barbecue sauce, then close the grill and cook until the ribs are cooked through, 15 to 20 minutes more.

12. Remove the ribs from the grill and let rest for 10 minutes. Slice the ribs and transfer to a large platter. Serve immediately with the reserved barbecue sauce and garnished with thyme sprigs.

CHERRY TOMATO SALAD

Kosher salt

2 pounds mixed summer beans, such as Romano, wax, or haricots verts

1 medium shallot, minced (¼ cup)

¼ cup sherry vinegar

1 tablespoon Dijon mustard

½ teaspoon freshly ground black pepper

½ cup extra-virgin olive oil

2 pounds mixed cherry tomatoes, halved

½ cup packed fresh basil leaves, large ones torn into 2 or 3 pieces

¼ cup lightly chopped fresh oregano leaves

1 bunch chives, cut into ¾-inch lengths (about ½ cup)

1. Bring a large pot of heavily salted water to a boil (the water should taste like the sea). Fill a large bowl with ice and water and set it nearby.

2. Drop the beans into the boiling water, one variety at a time, and blanch until each variety's color brightens and the beans are tender-crisp, about 1 minute per batch. Lift the beans from the water using tongs or a spider and plunge them into the ice bath. If you are using Romano beans, long beans, or any other extra-large variety, after cooking, cut them in half on an angle to match the size of the rest of the beans. Dry the beans on a large kitchen towel.

3. In a medium bowl, combine the shallot, vinegar, mustard, 2 teaspoons salt, and the pepper. While whisking, slowly pour in the olive oil and whisk until the oil is incorporated and the dressing is emulsified and creamy.

4. Toss the beans, tomatoes, basil, oregano, and chives in a large bowl. Pour half the dressing over the vegetables and toss to combine. Transfer to a large platter and drizzle with the remaining dressing just before serving.

SERVES 12

PREP TIME
15 minutes

ACTIVE TIME
20 minutes

TOTAL TIME
35 minutes

EASY

DIY SUNDAE BAR

1 quart vanilla ice cream

1 quart chocolate ice cream

1 quart "wild card" ice cream—
strawberry, or your favorite specialty
flavor

Classic Chocolate Sauce (recipe
follows)

Perfect Strawberry Sauce (recipe
follows)

Salted Caramel Sauce (recipe follows)

An assortment of toppings, such as:

NUTS
chopped toasted walnuts, pecans,
peanuts, hazelnuts, almonds

ADD-INS
rainbow sprinkles, crushed sourdough
pretzel bits, malt balls, granola, cacao
nibs, toasted coconut, chocolate-
covered coffee beans, sugar cereals,
mochi bits, chocolate shavings

FRUIT
cut-up strawberries, blueberries,
bananas, pineapple, blueberries,
raspberries, peaches, cherries

OVER THE TOP
brownie bits; crushed cookies
(chocolate chips, Oreos, Nutter
Butters, Thin Mints, shortbread); cake
crumbles; broken waffle cones

SODAS (FOR FLOATS!)
root beer, cola, grape soda, cream soda,
orange soda

1. Scoop the ice cream into eighteen jars, portioning about 5 ounces (2 or 3 scoops) per jar. You should have enough to fill about six jars per flavor. Feel free to mix it up and do a few jars Neapolitan-style. Put the lids on the jars and store in the freezer.

2. Meanwhile, set up your sundae bar: Set out sauces in squeeze bottles, arrange the toppings in small bowls, and put sodas (if using) on ice.

3. When ready to serve, set out a large bucket or tub filled with ice and nestle the mason jars of ice cream into the ice. Let the fun begin!

RECIPE CONTINUES

SERVES 18

PREP TIME
15 minutes

ACTIVE TIME
10 minutes

TOTAL TIME
25 minutes

MODERATE

Classic Chocolate Sauce

Makes 2 cups ◆ *Prep time:* 5 minutes
Active time: 10 minutes
Total time: 15 minutes ◆ *Easy*

1 cup bittersweet chocolate chunks (6 ounces)

3/4 cup heavy cream

2/3 cup light corn syrup

1/2 teaspoon kosher salt

1. Place the chocolate in a heatproof medium bowl and set aside.

2. In a small saucepan, combine the cream, corn syrup, and salt. Bring to a simmer over medium heat, stirring occasionally, and cook until the mixture starts to get frothy, 3 to 5 minutes; then remove from the heat.

3. Pour the hot cream mixture over the chocolate and stir with a rubber spatula or wooden spoon until the chocolate has melted and the mixture is completely smooth, 3 to 4 minutes. Let cool.

4. Transfer the cooled chocolate sauce into a squeeze bottle and use immediately or refrigerate until ready to use (if refrigerated, let the sauce come to room temperature on the counter for at least 1 hour before serving). The chocolate sauce will keep in the refrigerator for up to 1 month.

Perfect Strawberry Sauce

Makes 2 cups ◆ *Prep time:* 10 minutes
Active time: 40 minutes
Total time: 1 hour 10 minutes
(includes cooling time) ◆ *Easy*

1 pound strawberries, hulled and coarsely chopped (about 3 cups)

1 cup sugar

1/2 cup water

1 vanilla bean, split lengthwise and seeds scraped out

2 teaspoons fresh lemon juice

1. In a medium saucepan, combine the strawberries, sugar, water, and vanilla bean pod and seeds and bring to a boil over medium heat. Reduce the heat to maintain a simmer and cook, stirring occasionally, until the mixture has thickened and is slightly syrupy, about 30 minutes. Remove from the heat and let cool for about 20 minutes.

2. Transfer the strawberry mixture to a blender and puree until smooth. Add the lemon juice and pulse briefly to combine.

3. Pour the strawberry sauce into a squeeze bottle and use immediately, or refrigerate until ready to use. The strawberry sauce will keep in the refrigerator for up to 1 month.

Salted Caramel Sauce

Makes 2 cups ◆ *Prep time:* 5 minutes
Active time: 25 minutes
Total time: 1 hour *(includes cooling time)* ◆ *Easy*

2 cups sugar

1/4 cup water

2 teaspoons corn syrup

1 cup heavy cream

3/4 cup (1 1/2 sticks) unsalted butter, cut into small pieces, at room temperature

1 tablespoon kosher salt

1. In a medium saucepan, combine the sugar, water, and corn syrup. Cook over medium-high heat, being careful not to stir or disturb the contents of the pan until the mixture begins to boil. Allow the sugar mixture to cook until it reaches a deep, dark brown, 17 to 20 minutes, then immediately turn off the heat and, while whisking continuously, pour in the cream until incorporated. Be careful; the sugar syrup is extremely hot and the mixture will bubble up when the cream is added. While whisking, gradually add the butter and whisk until fully incorporated and you have a smooth, silky sauce. Stir in the salt and cool.

2. Pour the cooled caramel sauce into a squeeze bottle. Use immediately, or refrigerate until ready to use (if refrigerated, let the sauce come to room temperature on the counter for at least 1 hour before serving). The salted caramel sauce will keep in the refrigerator for up to 1 month.

HARVEST PARTY

Ring in the cooler weather with a get-together designed to celebrate the turning of the leaves, complete with a soul-satisfying buffet dinner that takes advantage of the fall bounty—and sends guests home with a jar of DIY pickles they can savor long after the night ends.

WHAT TO WEAR

Turtlenecks, fingerless gloves, plaid and flannel, cozy sweaters, jeans, overalls, trapper's hats.

PARTY BASICS

Cornstalks, autumn leaves, pumpkins, gourds, multicolored Indian corn. Rustic baskets and tin buckets for serving food.

PARTY UPGRADES

Set out carved-out gourds and pumpkins to house flowers and candles. Fill a galvanized tub with water and float carved-out apples and votives on top. Buy or rent a fire pit. To make your party look eclectic and fun, head to the thrift shop for mismatched plates and glasses (bring the kids along to help you hunt through bins of linens!). Use printed napkins.

OVER-THE-TOP IDEAS

Bring in bales of hay for seating. Craft or buy an oversize cornucopia (see the Host Craft Project) and fill it with fall produce. Buy or make handmade scarecrows. Spray leaves with assorted textured and colored paints.

WHAT GUESTS CAN BRING

Nuts, pumpkin seeds, popped popcorn, caramel corn, fall crudités (carrot sticks, broccoli, cauliflower, radishes, peppers, green beans), hummus (extra credit for the fall-hued roasted red pepper variety!), plastic jugs of cider, apples and caramel dip, flannel blankets.

GET GUESTS INVOLVED

Rally the troops to bring snacks, dessert, or a bag of apples. Hold back on putting out some table décor items so people can customize the tables for themselves. Ask guests to build the fire, set up the bobbing-for-apples station, light candles, plate food, and arrange the DIY pickle-jarring station (see page 146 for instructions). Children can pass out small servings of pickles or appetizers.

THE TABLE

Line your table with burlap or an autumn-hued tablecloth. Scatter gathered leaves and branches over the table and decorate with small votive candles.

THE FLOWERS

Autumn-colored mums, fireweed branches, sunflowers.

THE DRINKS

Keep a pot of warm apple cider simmering over low heat on the stove. Add whole cinnamon sticks and cloves for even more flavor. For the adults, add spiced rum or bourbon to the cider (or keep a bottle nearby so they can spike their own drinks). Fill a wheelbarrow with ice and chill bottles of old-fashioned root beer, ginger beer, and seasonal ales. Serve mulled wine, simmered with cloves, cinnamon, and orange slices, from a stockpot or slow cooker.

PLAN AHEAD

- *Three Days Before:* Make the spice rub, the barbecue sauce, and the mustard dressing.
- *Two Days Before:* Make your pickles. Grate your Parmesan.
- *One Day Before:* Bake the pear squares. Rub and wrap the pork butt.

ACTIVITIES

Bobbing for apples, raking leaves, pumpkin bowling, candy corn ring toss, waxed leaves, mason jars with pressed leaves.

PLAYLIST

"Harvest Moon," Neil Young

"Autumn Leaves," Nat King Cole

"September,"
Earth, Wind and Fire

"Harvest for the World,"
The Isley Brothers

"Pale September," Fiona Apple

"September Song," Frank Sinatra

"Autumn in New York,"
Ella Fitzgerald and
Louis Armstrong

"Autumn Serenade,"
John Coltrane

"The Last Day of Summer,"
The Cure

"Autumn Leaves," Ed Sheeran

"Autumn Almanac," The Kinks

"November Rain," Guns N' Roses

"Autumn Sweater," Yo La Tengo

PARTY PROJECT

Ask everyone to bring their end-of-summer produce bounty for pickling (with you providing backup produce for those who forgot). Keep extra brine hot in a slow cooker, then invite guests to pack mason jars with veggies and pour the brine over them for a quick-pickled takeaway they can pop into the fridge when they get home.

GIFTS FOR GUESTS

A take-home crock of pickles. Autumn-scented candles. A sachet of potpourri. A bag of Pumpkin Seed Bar Mix (page 170) with the recipe attached.

KEEP THE PARTY GOING

Organize a leaf-pile race in the backyard Divide the guests into teams, scatter leaves all over the yard, and set a timer. At the end, the team that creates the largest pile of leaves wins!

HOST CRAFT PROJECT
CORNUCOPIA

Shape chicken wire into the frame of a cornucopia of your desired size. Cover the chicken wire with papier-mâché (or masking tape), then hot-glue and wrap raffia or burlap around it...and voilà! *For instructions on how to make this cornucopia, go to DavidBurtka.com.*

QUICK AUTUMN PICKLES

◆ A N D ◆

DIY PICKLE BRINE

12 ounces yellow wax beans, ends snapped and discarded, or other vegetables of choice

1 cup white wine vinegar

2 dried bay leaves, broken in half

2 tablespoons sugar

1½ teaspoons whole black peppercorns

1 teaspoon coriander seeds

1 tablespoon kosher salt

1 cup water

1. Pack the beans upright into a heatproof 24-ounce glass canning jar with a tight-fitting lid.

2. In a medium saucepan, combine the vinegar, bay leaves, sugar, peppercorns, coriander, salt, and water and bring to a boil over medium heat, stirring occasionally to make sure the sugar and salt dissolve completely, about 5 minutes.

3. Pour the brine over the beans so the beans are completely submerged in the liquid. If they're not, use a spoon to gently press them down below the level of the liquid. Let cool for 20 minutes, cover the jar with a tight-fitting lid, and refrigerate for up to 2 weeks.

MAKES ONE
24-ounce
jar of pickles

PREP TIME
10 minutes

ACTIVE TIME
5 minutes

TOTAL TIME
1 hour 30 minutes

EASY

◆

Send friends home with these DIY treats!

While I suggest pickling most of these vegetables raw, submerging the okra in boiling water for a few minutes makes it less slimy.

OTHER VEGETABLES
YOU CAN USE

Carrots ◆ Cauliflower ◆ Cucumbers
Okra ◆ Radishes ◆ Zucchini

BARBECUE PORK SLIDERS

2 tablespoons cumin seeds

2 tablespoons coriander seeds

⅓ cup lightly packed dark brown sugar

3 tablespoons smoked paprika

2 tablespoons granulated garlic

2 tablespoons dry mustard powder

1½ teaspoons ancho chile powder

2 tablespoons kosher salt

½ teaspoon freshly ground black pepper

1 (8-pound) boneless pork butt

4 to 6 cups barbecue sauce, store-bought or homemade (recipe follows)

16 potato slider buns, lightly toasted

SPECIAL EQUIPMENT
spice grinder or mortar and pestle

1. In a small dry skillet, toast the cumin and coriander seeds over medium heat, swirling the pan occasionally, until fragrant, 2½ to 3 minutes. Turn off the heat and transfer the spices to a small plate to cool, then finely grind them in a spice grinder or using a mortar and pestle.

2. Transfer the ground toasted spices to a medium bowl and whisk in the brown sugar, paprika, granulated garlic, dry mustard powder, ancho chile powder, salt, and black pepper.

3. Place the pork butt in a large bowl and rub half the spice blend over it, adding more as needed to evenly coat all sides and surfaces of the pork (save any unused spice blend in a jar or resealable plastic bag for another use). Wrap the pork butt in plastic wrap so it is completely sealed, return it to the bowl, and refrigerate for at least 4 hours or up to overnight.

4. When ready to cook the pork, preheat the oven to 250°F.

5. Unwrap the pork butt (discard the plastic) and place it in a roasting pan. Let it come to room temperature for 30 minutes. Transfer the pan to the oven and cook until you can stick a fork into the meat and easily break off a chunk, about 8 hours. Remove the pan from the oven, remove and discard any large pieces of fat from the pork, and break the pork into 4 to 6 large chunks. Return the pan to the oven and cook until a fork easily shreds the meat, 2 hours 30 minutes to 3 hours more.

6. Remove the pan from the oven and shred the pork with two forks, letting the meat fall into the fat and juices in the pan.

7. Place the roasting pan over a burner on the stovetop and turn the heat to medium-high. Cook the pork in the residual pork fat, stirring occasionally, until the meat is lightly crispy in spots, 8 to 10 minutes. Turn off the heat, then stir in as little or as much barbecue sauce as you like.

8. Divide the meat among the buns. Serve with any remaining barbecue sauce on the side.

MAKES 16 SLIDERS

PREP TIME
15 minutes

ACTIVE TIME
25 minutes

TOTAL TIME
15 hours
10 minutes
(includes time for marinating and cooking the pork butt)

MODERATE

Make this pork up to **three days in advance** to save yourself time and cleanup on party day.

Barbecue Sauce

Makes 8 cups   ◆   *Prep time:* 5 minutes
Active time: 15 minutes   ◆
Total time: 20 minutes   ◆   *Easy*

2 cups ketchup

2 cups lightly packed dark brown sugar

1 cup apple cider vinegar

1 cup unsulfured molasses

1 cup canned tomato sauce

½ cup tomato paste

¼ cup of your favorite hot sauce

2 tablespoons liquid smoke

2 tablespoons Worcestershire sauce

2 tablespoons garlic powder

1 tablespoon yellow mustard

1 tablespoon ancho chile powder

1. In a medium saucepan, whisk together the ketchup, brown sugar, vinegar, molasses, tomato sauce, tomato paste, hot sauce, liquid smoke, Worcestershire sauce, garlic powder, mustard, and ancho chile powder and bring to a boil over medium-high heat.

2. Reduce the heat to medium and simmer, stirring often, until the sauce is thick and glossy, about 15 minutes. Transfer to an airtight container and refrigerate for up to 1 month.

BRUSSELS SPROUT AND CHESTNUT SLAW

WITH MUSTARD DRESSING

Though we call for Honeycrisp, use your favorite apple here. Cutting the apple into fancy matchsticks is a great flourish, but plain thin slices work fine, too. If you prep the apples in advance, keep them in a bowl of lemony water or add vitamin C powder to avoid browning.

½ cup sherry vinegar

2 tablespoons whole-grain mustard

1 teaspoon celery seeds

Kosher salt and freshly ground black pepper

1 cup extra-virgin olive oil

1½ pounds large Brussels sprouts

3½ ounces roasted chestnuts, coarsely chopped (¾ cup)

3 large celery stalks, ends trimmed and stalks thinly sliced on an angle (about 1½ cups)

1 large sweet-tart apple, such as Honeycrisp, halved, cored, and thinly sliced into matchsticks

1. In a large bowl, whisk together the vinegar, mustard, celery seeds, a large pinch of salt, and a few twists of pepper until incorporated. While whisking, slowly drizzle in the olive oil and whisk until emulsified. Taste and season with salt and pepper; set aside.

2. If using a food processor to shred the Brussels sprouts, trim the ends from the sprouts and then pass them through the feed tube to thinly slice. If using a mandoline, leave the ends on the Brussels sprouts and, holding each one at the stem end, slice them on the mandoline from the top down; be careful not to get too close to the stem end—your fingertips are more important than a few extra shreds! Place the sliced sprouts in a large bowl and add the chestnuts, celery, and apple.

3. Pour half the dressing over the Brussels sprout mixture and toss to combine. Taste and season with more dressing, salt, and/or pepper. Let the slaw sit on the counter for 30 minutes to let the flavors meld before serving. Toss again and serve. (Any leftover dressing can be stored in an airtight container in the refrigerator for up to 2 weeks.)

SERVES 6 TO 8

PREP TIME
15 minutes

ACTIVE TIME
5 minutes

TOTAL TIME
50 minutes
(includes marinating time)

EASY

For serving, use a wooden bowl to bring a **farmhouse** vibe into the room.

VITAMIN C POWDER

This magic powder prevents food from turning brown for hours and is available at any health food store.

POTATO WEDGES

WITH PARMESAN

These are the potatoes you make for company. The three-step process involved in making them requires a little bit of patience, but it's sooo worth it. Soaking the potatoes to reduce the amount of starch yields nice fluffy potatoes with an extra-crispy exterior. Bringing the potatoes to a simmer very slowly in salted water seasons the potatoes from the inside out. Baking them in a super-hot oven gets them browned and crunchy. Prepare for these to disappear fast!

6 medium russet potatoes (about 4½ pounds)

½ cup (1 stick) salted butter

2 garlic cloves, lightly smashed

2 sprigs rosemary

Kosher salt

1 (4-ounce) wedge Parmesan cheese, finely grated (about 3 cups)

¼ cup fresh flat-leaf parsley leaves, coarsely chopped

1. Adjust one oven rack to the lower-third position and one to the upper-third position and preheat the oven to 450°F. Line two rimmed baking sheets with parchment paper.

2. Cut each potato in half lengthwise, then cut each half into 3 wedges. Place them in a large pot and cover with cold water; let rest for at least 10 minutes but no more than 20.

3. In a small saucepan, melt the butter halfway over medium heat, then add the garlic and rosemary sprigs and cook, swirling the pan often, until fragrant, about 5 minutes. Remove from the heat and set aside.

4. Drain the potatoes and refill the pot with enough cold water to cover them by 1 inch. Season the water liberally with salt (the water should taste like the sea) and bring the water to a slow simmer over medium heat. Cook the potatoes until al dente, about 10 minutes from the time the water starts to simmer. Drain in a large colander, then divide the potatoes between the two prepared baking sheets, arranging them in a single layer and leaving at least ½ inch between each wedge.

5. Strain the garlic-rosemary butter through a fine-mesh sieve into a small bowl; discard the solids. Use a pastry brush to brush half the butter onto the potato wedges.

6. Bake until light golden brown and crispy, about 25 minutes, flipping the potatoes midway through cooking and rotating the pans top to bottom and front to back. Remove the baking sheets from the oven, brush the remaining garlic-rosemary butter onto the potatoes, and sprinkle a generous amount of the Parmesan on all sides. Return the potatoes to the oven and bake until the cheese is light golden brown, about 10 minutes (remove them earlier if they seem like they are beginning to burn).

7. Remove the potatoes from the oven and let cool for at least 5 minutes before serving; as they cool, the cheese will crisp up just like a Parmesan frico (a lacy cheese cracker). Transfer the potato wedges (and any extra frico pieces from the baking sheet) to a large platter, garnish with the parsley, and serve.

SERVES 6 TO 8

PREP TIME
20 minutes

ACTIVE TIME
1 hour 40 minutes

TOTAL TIME
2 hours 10 minutes

MODERATE

Parchment paper helps prevent these little shards from burning. **Sprinkling extra cheese** on the paper creates crispy, **frico-style** cheese crackers.

PEAR SQUARES

There's nothing more special than cooking from a family recipe! This is a take on my grandma's apple square recipe, which blends lard with butter and lemon juice in the crust for extra-flaky results. I swapped in juicy pears, which really say "autumn" to me.

FOR THE CRUST

4½ cups all-purpose flour, plus more for dusting

3 tablespoons granulated sugar

1½ teaspoons fine sea salt

1 cup (2 sticks) unsalted butter, frozen

1 cup lard (about 8 ounces), frozen

2 to 3 tablespoons fresh lemon juice

FOR THE FILLING

10 ripe Bartlett pears (about 5 pounds), or 10 apples, such as Honeycrisp or Granny Smith

2 tablespoons fresh lemon juice

⅔ cup granulated sugar

¼ cup all-purpose flour

1 cup ground gingersnap cookies, store-bought or homemade (see page 171)

FOR THE GLAZE

1 cup confectioners' sugar

2 tablespoons water

½ teaspoon vanilla extract

1. Make the crust: In a large bowl, whisk together the flour, sugar, and salt. Set a box grater over the flour mixture and grate the butter and the lard on the medium-size holes directly into the dry ingredients. Use your fingers to rub the fat into the flour until the mixture resembles coarse, pea-size crumbs.

2. Fill a large glass with about ½ cup water, add some ice to the glass, and let the water chill for a few minutes. Remove the ice cubes from the water, pour off any extra water so you have ½ cup, and add the lemon juice. Pour the lemon water into the dry ingredients and use your hands to stir until the mixture forms a shaggy dough that holds together when pressed (stir in up to ¼ cup of additional cold water, 1 tablespoon at a time, as needed).

3. Turn the dough out onto a lightly floured work surface and knead until it just comes together, 3 to 4 minutes. Set the dough on a large sheet of plastic wrap and press it into a 9-inch square, about 1 inch thick. Seal tightly in the plastic wrap and refrigerate for at least 1 hour or up to a week, or freeze for up to 2 weeks (thaw in the fridge overnight before using).

4. Make the filling: Peel, halve, core, and slice the pears lengthwise into paper-thin slices. Transfer to a large bowl and toss with the lemon juice to prevent browning. Toss with the granulated sugar and flour and set aside.

5. Preheat the oven to 350°F.

MAKES 24 SQUARES

PREP TIME
15 minutes

ACTIVE TIME
45 minutes

TOTAL TIME
6 hours
55 minutes
(includes chilling, baking, and cooling time)

INVOLVED

If you've only got **apples**, use those instead! It'll be just as delish.

6. Roll out the chilled dough on a lightly floured work surface into a 20 by 15-inch rectangle, about ¼ inch thick. Carefully roll the dough around the rolling pin to make it easy to lift and unroll it over a 12 by 18-inch rimmed baking sheet (if the dough tears slightly, that's okay; just press it back together). Press the dough into the bottom and up the sides of the pan, pressing any cracks together (it's a very forgiving dough). Trim off any dough hanging over the sides of the pan. Sprinkle the ground gingersnap cookies evenly over the dough and layer the pears horizontally over the gingersnap crumbs. Bake until the crust is golden brown and pulls away from the edges of the pan and the pears are tender, about 1 hour 10 minutes, rotating the pan every 20 minutes.

7. Right before the squares are done baking, make the glaze: In a medium bowl, whisk together the confectioners' sugar, water, and vanilla until smooth.

8. Remove the pear squares from the oven and set the baking sheet over a wire rack. Drizzle the glaze evenly over the top and let cool completely, about 4 hours. Once cooled, cut into 24 squares. The squares keep, covered, for 1 week in the refrigerator or for 4 to 6 months in the freezer, tightly wrapped.

PUMPKIN-CARVING BRUNCH

Halloween isn't all about spooky! Take the opportunity to turn it into a friendly affair without the scare. Since you were destined to carve pumpkins anyway, why not make a party out of it? A fun, crafty brunch is a great way to get your kids and their friends together during one of those pitch-perfect pre-Halloween autumnal weekends. Time to decorate with silly, silly ghosts and friendly monsters. Wherever you set up—inside or outside—just make sure there's enough room for everyone to spread out and express their artistic side.

PARTY BASICS

Have two separate areas, one for the food and one for the carving…and never the two shall meet! Have all your tools—plus pens or pencils—in mason jars or cups. Scatter tracing templates all around the space. Because these are kids' activities, use plastic *everything* if you can! Have baby wipes and big rolls of paper towels at the ready, as well as plastic bags for discarding leftover pieces of pumpkin.

PARTY UPGRADES

Set up a "seed and gut" roasting station where kids can help separate pumpkin seeds from innards before you squire them away for salting, seasoning, and roasting with flavors like sugar and cinnamon, curry powder, and garlic salt. Create jack-o'-lantern garlands by hanging cobwebs and orange helium balloons. Make jack-o'-lantern faces with a permanent marker, and make faux pumpkins out of clementines and celery stalks. Peel clementines and add a small cut stick of celery for the top of the stalk. Send people home with takeaway caramel apple–making kits complete with twigs, wrapped caramels, and apples in brown paper bags adorned with pumpkin stickers.

OVER-THE-TOP IDEAS

Set up a Halloween candy bar complete with brown paper bags cut out to look like jack-o'-lantern faces. Spray your pumpkins with glow-in-the-dark spray paint. Create a pumpkin-themed photo booth with seasonal props like jagged teeth and scary masks (Etsy has a lot of great harvest stuff for sale). Supply cookie cutters to cut out the outside of the pumpkin and dry-erase markers so people can take their pumpkin carving to the next level. Get battery-operated candles (surprisingly affordable at big-box stores) and fake votives for people to take home.

WHAT GUESTS CAN BRING
A pumpkin (preferably hollowed out at home). A bag of apples or clementines, or candy. Apple cider doughnuts. Celery sticks. Pumpkin-carving tools (though you should have extras on hand).

GET GUESTS INVOLVED
Have guests line tables with newspapers and put carving tools into mason jars. For the baked apples, have them core apples with a teaspoon. Ask kids to fill small cups with Pumpkin Seed Bar Mix. Direct each person to stake out their own place at the carving table. Ask kids to sort seeds from pumpkin guts for roasting, and get them to set up the pumpkin-carving station and clean up the trash.

WHAT TO WEAR
Clothes you don't mind getting dirty. A costume (optional!). Monster teeth!

THE TABLE
Pumpkin carving can get messy, so cover the table with a tarp or newspaper. For décor, go for full-on fun for the kids: orange or black tablecloths covered with fall foliage, pumpkins, and gourds.

THE FLOWERS
Orange and black mums in vases, carnations sprayed orange and black and decorated with plastic black and orange spiders.

THE DRINKS
Inaugurate pumpkin-spice season with a bottle of pumpkin-spice syrup for lattes or flavored steamed milk. Serve hot and cold apple cider, apple juice, and pumpkin ale.

PLAN AHEAD
- *Three Days Before:* Make the apple streusel topping and the Pumpkin Seed Bar Mix.
- *Two Days Before:* Make the mulled cider.
- *One Day Before:* Make all elements of the Pumpkin Parfaits, then assemble them day-of.

ACTIVITIES
Pass out pumpkin-carving templates to inspire creativity. Save the pumpkin seeds and roast them in the oven.

PARTY PROJECT
Pumpkin Favors: Cut orange tissue paper into circles, fill the centers with candy, pull up the sides, and use green painter's tape to create height and shape into a "stem."

GIFTS FOR GUESTS
Autumn-inspired and -flavored foods such as pumpkin popcorn, chai, candy, and chocolate.

PLAYLIST

"Monster Mash," Misfits

"I Want Candy," Bow Wow Wow

"Ghostbusters," Ray Parker Jr.

"Black Cat," Janet Jackson

"Beetlejuice," Danny Elfman

"A Nightmare on My Street," DJ Jazzy Jeff

"The Addams Family," TV Themes

"Time Warp," *The Rocky Horror Picture Show*

"Sugar," Robin Schultz

"Love Potion Number 9," The Searchers

"Toxic," Britney Spears

"Superstition," Stevie Wonder

"Witchcraft," Frank Sinatra

KEEP THE PARTY GOING
Gather everyone around the TV for a screening of *It's the Great Pumpkin, Charlie Brown.*

Use **dry-erase markers** to design pumpkin faces.

MULLED CIDER

WITH GINGER AND CARDAMOM

14 cinnamon sticks

16 whole green cardamom pods

20 whole cloves

1 (2-inch) piece fresh ginger, peeled and thinly sliced

1 cup lightly packed light brown sugar

1 gallon apple cider

Spiced rum or bourbon (optional)

1. Preheat the oven to 350°F.

2. Place the cinnamon sticks, cardamom pods, and cloves on a small rimmed baking sheet and toast in the oven until the spices become fragrant, 6 to 7 minutes. Transfer the toasted spices to a large pot.

3. Add the ginger, brown sugar, and apple cider to the pot. Bring to a boil over medium-high heat, reduce the heat to medium-low, cover, and simmer, stirring occasionally, until the apple cider is infused with the ginger and spices, 2 hours 30 minutes.

4. Ladle the cider into mugs; adults might spike their own with a splash of spiced rum or bourbon if the mood strikes.

SERVES 16

PREP TIME
5 minutes

ACTIVE TIME
10 minutes

TOTAL TIME
2 hours 45 minutes

EASY

BAKED APPLES

My daughter, Harper, doesn't love apples, but she can't resist these! You can prestuff them, then cook them before school for a great (and relatively healthy) breakfast. The bigger the apple, the better—that means more room for filling!

6 medium Honeycrisp apples (about 3 pounds)

½ teaspoon ground cinnamon

¼ teaspoon ground ginger

½ teaspoon kosher salt

½ cup lightly packed light brown sugar

1 cup unsweetened vanilla almond milk

1 cup plus 2 tablespoons old-fashioned rolled oats

4 tablespoons (½ stick) unsalted butter

⅓ cup chopped pecans

1 tablespoon all-purpose flour

¾ cup apple cider

1. Preheat the oven to 375°F.

2. Cut ½ inch off the top of each apple. Use a small spoon to scoop out the flesh of the apples, leaving ¼ inch on all sides and the bottom so you have an empty apple "cup." Put the scooped apple flesh in a medium bowl and set aside. Place the apple cups in a 7 by 11-inch baking dish.

3. Turn the apple flesh out onto a cutting board and remove and discard the seeds and cores. Finely chop enough of the scooped apple flesh to equal 1 cup (save any remaining apple flesh for another use) and return it to the bowl. Stir in ¼ teaspoon of the cinnamon, the ginger, ¼ teaspoon of the salt, 2 tablespoons of the brown sugar, the almond milk, and ¾ cup of the oats. Fill the apples almost to the top with the filling.

4. In a small skillet, melt 2 tablespoons of the butter over medium heat and cook the melted butter until it starts to bubble and foam, swirling the butter in the pan occasionally, about 2 minutes. Cook, stirring continuously, until the foam subsides and brown flecks start to appear, about 1 minute more. Pour the browned butter into a medium bowl (set the pan aside for later) and stir in the pecans, flour, and the remaining oats, brown sugar, cinnamon, and salt. Divide the streusel topping evenly over the apples.

5. Cut the remaining 2 tablespoons butter into small cubes and scatter them around the apples in the baking dish, then pour in the apple cider. Bake, uncovered, basting the apples (but not the streusel) with the cider sauce and rotating the baking dish every 15 minutes, until the apples are completely tender and the streusel is golden brown, about 45 minutes. If the streusel browns before the apples are tender, cover the dish loosely with a piece of aluminum foil.

6. Remove the apples from the oven and transfer to a large serving platter.

7. Pour the juices from the baking dish into the reserved skillet and bring to a boil over medium-high heat. Reduce the heat to maintain a simmer and cook until the mixture has reduced slightly and is the consistency of thin gravy, about 5 minutes. Drizzle the sauce over the apples and serve.

SERVES 6

PREP TIME
10 minutes

ACTIVE TIME
35 minutes

TOTAL TIME
1 hour 30 minutes

MODERATE

Choose apples with **flat bottoms** so they stand well when filled. **Honeycrisp** and **Fuji** apples work well here, too.

HAM, EGG, AND CHEESE
CALZONES

All-purpose flour, for dusting

4 ounces thinly sliced black forest ham (about 8 slices), diced

2 cups shredded cheddar cheese (8 ounces)

3 large eggs

Kosher salt and freshly ground black pepper

1 pound prepared pizza dough, at room temperature

Olive oil, for brushing

Hot sauce and/or salsa, for serving

1. Set one oven rack in the bottom third of the oven and one rack in the upper third and preheat the oven to 450°F. Line two rimmed baking sheets with parchment paper. Set out another piece of parchment paper, lightly floured, on a flat work surface.

2. Combine the ham and cheese in a medium bowl and set aside. In a small bowl, whisk the eggs with a large pinch each of salt and pepper.

3. Place a bowl of room-temperature water on the counter. Place the dough on a lightly floured work surface and divide it into 8 equal pieces. Cover all but one piece of dough with a damp dish towel.

4. Place the uncovered piece of dough on the floured parchment paper. Use a rolling pin to roll the dough into a very thin 8-inch round and carefully transfer the round to one of the prepared baking sheets. Use a pastry brush (or your finger) to dab water on the edge of half the circle. On that same water-brushed side, place a heaping ¼ cup of the ham-cheese mixture on the center of the dough. Form a well in the center of the ham-cheese mound and spoon in 1½ to 2 tablespoons of the seasoned eggs, to come up right below the top of the ham-cheese mixture. Carefully fold the unfilled side of the dough over the filling and use your fingers to press the edges together, then fold them over so that the calzone is tightly crimped. Repeat the process with the remaining pieces of dough and the filling so that you end up with 4 calzones on each baking sheet (if any egg seeps out of the calzones, that's okay; you can trim it off after baking).

5. Brush the calzones with olive oil and bake until they're golden brown and crispy, rotating the baking sheets from top to bottom and front to back once halfway through baking, about 10 minutes. Remove from the oven and let the calzones cool on the baking sheets for 5 minutes, then transfer to a platter and serve with hot sauce and/or salsa.

MAKES 8 CALZONES

PREP TIME
10 minutes

ACTIVE TIME
20 minutes

TOTAL TIME
45 minutes
(includes cooling time)

MODERATE

Another great **make-ahead recipe**! Keep the baked calzones in the fridge, then pop them into the oven at 350°F for 10 minutes and serve with salsa and/or hot sauce.

PUMPKIN SEED BAR MIX

1 cup (2 sticks) unsalted butter

4 garlic cloves, finely minced

½ teaspoon onion powder

½ teaspoon smoked paprika

¼ teaspoon ground cumin

1 teaspoon kosher salt

4 dashes of hot sauce

¼ cup Worcestershire sauce

4 cups raw pumpkin seeds

3 cups miniature square pretzels or miniature pretzel twists

3 cups store-bought sesame stick snacks

2 cups plain toasted corn kernels (such as Corn Nuts)

2 cups raw walnut halves or pieces, hulled sunflower seeds, or crispy corn snacks, such as Bugles

This addictive recipe is a fantastic way to use up all the extra seeds we all seem to have around during pumpkin-carving season. But if you want to make it during other times of the year, try buying salted roasted pumpkin seeds from a specialty store (just remember to adjust the salt in the recipe accordingly so your mix doesn't taste like a salt lick). If you're allergic to walnuts, you can substitute hulled sunflower seeds.

1. Adjust the oven racks to the lower-third and upper-third positions and preheat the oven to 300°F. Line two baking sheets with parchment paper.

2. In a small saucepan, heat the butter and garlic over medium heat, swirling the pan occasionally, until the butter has melted, 2 to 3 minutes. Turn off the heat, set aside to cool for 5 minutes, then stir in the onion powder, paprika, cumin, salt, hot sauce, and Worcestershire sauce.

3. In a large bowl, combine the pumpkin seeds, pretzels, sesame sticks, corn kernels, and walnuts. Add the butter mixture and use your hands to gently mix until everything is thoroughly coated.

4. Transfer the mixture to the prepared baking sheets and bake until the pumpkin seeds and walnuts are lightly toasted and the mixture is mostly dry, about 1 hour, stirring every 10 minutes. Remove from the oven and let the mix cool completely on the baking sheets. The mix can be stored in zip-top bags or other airtight containers at room temperature for 1 to 2 months.

Tip *If using seeds scooped from a pumpkin, you'll need seeds from 2 or 3 large pumpkins. To prepare the pumpkin seeds, rinse them well, removing all pumpkin fibers, pat them dry, spread them into an even layer on a rimmed baking sheet, and roast them in a preheated 300°F oven until dry, 9 to 10 minutes.*

MAKES ABOUT 14 CUPS
—
recipe can be halved

PREP TIME
10 minutes

ACTIVE TIME
20 minutes

TOTAL TIME
3 hours 35 minutes
(includes baking and cooling time)

EASY

PUMPKIN PARFAITS

WITH HOMEMADE GINGERSNAPS

These are a great activity for kids: Stretch out a lazy day by having them help make the cookies and assemble these decadent desserts. They're so rich, three or four bites just might be enough.

FOR THE GINGERSNAPS

2 cups all-purpose flour, plus more for dusting

¾ cup granulated sugar

1 teaspoon ground cinnamon

1 teaspoon ground ginger

1 teaspoon baking soda

½ teaspoon ground cloves

½ teaspoon fine sea salt

¼ teaspoon ground allspice

¾ cup (1½ sticks) unsalted butter

1 (2-inch) piece fresh ginger, peeled and finely grated (about 1 heaping tablespoon)

¼ cup unsulfured molasses

1 large egg

⅓ cup turbinado sugar, such as Sugar In The Raw

FOR THE PUMPKIN MOUSSE

¼ cup confectioners' sugar

1½ cups heavy cream

½ cup mascarpone cheese (4 ounces)

2 tablespoons pure maple syrup

1 cup pure pumpkin puree (not pumpkin pie filling)

SPECIAL EQUIPMENT

1¾-inch-wide pumpkin-shaped cookie cutter

1. Make the cookie dough: In a large bowl, whisk together the flour, granulated sugar, cinnamon, ground ginger, baking soda, cloves, salt, and allspice.

2. In a medium skillet, melt the butter over medium heat and cook, swirling the pan often, until it starts to bubble and foam, about 3 minutes. Cook, stirring continuously, until brown flecks appear, about 2 minutes more.

3. Pour the browned butter into a medium bowl and whisk in the grated ginger and molasses. Let cool for 15 minutes, whisking occasionally, then whisk in the egg. Pour the butter mixture into the dry ingredients and use a wooden spoon to stir until just combined. Flatten the dough into a disc, wrap it in plastic wrap, and refrigerate for at least 1 hour and up to 4 days. (The dough can also be frozen for up to 2 weeks, then defrosted in the refrigerator 4 hours before baking.)

4. Preheat the oven to 350°F. Line a large baking sheet with parchment paper.

5. Dust a clean work surface with flour, then roll half the cookie dough into a ¼-inch-thick sheet. Use a 1¾-inch-wide pumpkin-shaped cookie cutter to cut out 16 small pumpkins; reserve the scraps. Place the cookies on the prepared baking sheet, leaving ½ inch between each. Place the baking sheet in the refrigerator while you roll out the rest of the dough.

6. Press the dough scraps into the other half of the cookie dough. Place a piece of parchment paper the same size as a baking sheet on your work surface and roll the dough directly on the parchment into a ¼-inch-thick round. Slide the parchment onto a second baking sheet (you aren't cutting cookies out of this portion). Remove the baking sheet from the refrigerator and sprinkle the cut cookies and the uncut dough round with the turbinado sugar.

RECIPE CONTINUES

SERVES 8

makes 16 cookies, plus extra for crumbling, and 5 cups mousse

PREP TIME
15 minutes

ACTIVE TIME
45 minutes

TOTAL TIME
4 hours
35 minutes
(includes chilling, baking, and cooling time)

MODERATE

These **cookies are so good**, you may want to make them as a **stand-alone recipe**.

7. Place the baking sheet with the uncut dough round on the lower rack and the cut cookies on the upper rack and bake for 15 minutes, rotating the pans front to back midway through baking, until the cookies have puffed and no longer feel tacky. Remove the baking sheet with the cookies from the oven and move the large uncut cookie to the upper rack; set the sheet of cookies on a wire rack and let cool. Bake the large uncut cookie until puffed and no longer tacky, about 10 minutes more. Remove the baking sheet from the oven, set it on a wire rack, and let the large cookie cool completely, about 2 hours.

8. Break the baked cookie round into large pieces and put the pieces in a large resealable plastic bag. Seal the bag and use a rolling pin to crush the cookie pieces into fine crumbs. (Get the kids to do this!) You should get about 4 cups crumbs. You can also use a food processor to pulse the cookie pieces into crumbs.

9. Make the pumpkin mousse: Sift the confectioners' sugar into the bowl of a stand mixer. Add the cream and use the whisk attachment to whip on medium speed until the cream forms medium peaks, 3 to 4 minutes. Add the mascarpone and whip until the cream forms stiff peaks, 1 to 2 minutes more. Transfer half the mascarpone whipped cream to a medium bowl and set aside. Add the maple syrup and pumpkin to the mixer bowl and whip until it forms stiff peaks, 1 to 2 minutes.

10. Make the parfaits: In eight short 8-ounce juice glasses, layer 3 scant tablespoons of the pumpkin mousse, 2 heaping tablespoons of the cookie crumbs, 3 tablespoons of the whipped mascarpone cream, 2 heaping tablespoons of the cookie crumbs, 3 scant tablespoons of the pumpkin mousse, and about 1 tablespoon of the mascarpone whipped cream. Top each with a pumpkin-shaped cookie and serve.

FRIGHT NIGHT!

Boo! This dark and spooky Halloween get-together is most definitely adults-only (all witches, wolves, vampires, mummies—and anyone else skipping out on the trick-or-treating—are welcome as well). Pick a weekend evening near Halloween, turn the lights down low, and prepare for a devilishly delicious night.

Halloween was always a big deal as a kid, but it wasn't until I met Neil that it became an amazing annual event. Neil showed me that just trick-or-treating was for amateurs—why just give out candy when you can host a blowout complete with entertainment, gruesome food, actors dressed as ghouls and goblins, even a DJ to blast the "Monster Mash"! We've had some epic parties over the years.

WHAT GUESTS CAN BRING
A trick-or-treat, favorite ghost story, or costume.

GET GUESTS INVOLVED
Ask people to help shake the cocktails. Have someone adjust the lighting or light candles to set the mood. Guests can also help scatter fake bugs all over the table, set the table, arrange the flowers, and set up the props for the photo booth.

WHAT TO WEAR
This is a costume for a fright night to remember, so tell everyone to wear their creepy-craziest, most elaborate and inspired outfit. Just make sure it's comfortable for sitting down! Word to the wise: Masks, makeup, and fake teeth might make it tricky to eat.

THE TABLE
Set up clusters of flickering black and bloodred candles. Fill candelabras with burning candles that drip down to create the ultimate sexy, spooky Halloween party vibe. Lay out black and silver flatware settings. Cover the table with fake bugs, rats, bats, eyeballs, body parts—in this case, the more gruesome the better.

THE FLOWERS
Save or collect dead flowers from friends, then arrange them in bouquets. Spray-paint them black, then cover them with cobwebs and bugs. Arrange the flowers in skull-shaped vases and use quirkily shaped cockscomb flowers for "brains."

PARTY BASICS

Cover the table with a black tablecloth and black napkins. Wrap "cobwebs" around light fixtures. Place lots of candles and candelabras everywhere!

PARTY UPGRADES

Purchase mismatched vases and candlesticks at your local thrift shop; give old wine bottles new life by spray-painting them black. Mark each place setting with a fake skeleton hand holding the guest's name card. For your playlist, add in spooky sounds like a witch's cackle or a door creaking between songs.

OVER-THE-TOP IDEAS

Set the table with varying shades of black dinnerware and accessories so that place mats, charger plates, dinner plates, and wineglasses become active parts of the décor. Accent with centerpieces made of black tree branches, black orchids, and brass candelabras. Fill your living room with funeral flowers. Rent a casket and stage a photo shoot where guests can pose next to (or inside!) it. Hire a waiter who's willing to dress and be made up as a dead butler. You can also have the "butler" plan various scary surprises during the night.

THE DRINKS
Apple cider, To-Kill-Ya Martinis, nonalcoholic punch in a punch bowl set inside a larger plastic bowl filled with dry ice and warm water so the punch is spooky and smoking (every now and then, add warm water to the dry ice bowl).

PLAN AHEAD
- *Three Days Before:* Make the dumplings, chile sauce, barbecue sauce, and salad dressing.
- *Two Days Before:* Roast the squash and make the soup.
- *One Day Before:* Prepare the ribs and the bomboloni dough.

BLOODY CANDLE TAPERS

Take cheap red wax tapers and melt them all over the top of thicker, funeral home–style white candles until the red wax drips onto and down the white candles, making them look like they're dripping "blood." Extra credit for studs, nails, and barbed wire stuck into the white candles!

GIFTS FOR GUESTS

Vintage copies of *Frankenstein* or other classics. Candy blood and IV bags. Dried crickets or larvae snacks. Horror trading cards. Pentagram chains. Voodoo dolls. A monster-killing kit ("holy water," garlic, wooden stakes, crucifix, and silver bullets).

KEEP THE PARTY GOING

Set up a costume photo booth with an instant camera. Recruit a musician friend to dress up like a zombie and play an instrument for a spooky concert. Screen a horror movie. Tell scary stories by candlelight.

HOST CRAFT PROJECT

Purchase mason jars with lids, a glue gun, plastic snakes, fake bugs, bloody fake fingers, eyeballs (or any other creepy accessories), water, and food coloring. Glue faux rat tails to the tops of the mason jar lids (so when you screw the top on, they hang down the jar) and glue the rest of the props to the inside of the jars. Let them dry, then fill with water and a few drops of your desired food coloring (green and bright yellow work best) for a creepy take-home jar.

ACTIVITIES

Hire a tarot card reader and a fortune-teller. Set up a Ouija board for spooky fun or plan a fake séance. Tell ghost stories, watch a scary movie, or find a haunted house in your area.

PARTY PROJECT

Pass out index cards to your guests. Have each guest write down the most gruesome way to die in detail. Have everyone hand their ideas to you, then shuffle the cards and read them out loud, so your guests can guess who wrote what.

PLAYLIST

"I Put a Spell on You," Nina Simone

"Theme from *Halloween*," Horror Movie Theme Orchestra

"Black Magic Woman," Santana

"Cry Little Sister (Theme from *Lost Boys*)," Gerard McMann

"Dark Horse," Katy Perry

"Highway to Hell," AC/DC

"Spooky," Dusty Springfield

"Sympathy for the Devil," Rolling Stones

"Theme from *American Horror Story*," Horror Movie Theme Orchestra

"Zombie," The Cranberries

"Thriller," Michael Jackson

"Bad Moon Rising," Creedence Clearwater Revival

TO-KILL-YA MARTINIS

WITH LEAKY LYCHEES

Tequila with Bloody Eyeballs

1/4 cup cranberries (about 24 total)

2 tablespoons grenadine, plus more for drizzling

12 canned lychees in syrup, drained

3/4 cup sugar

3/4 cup water

1/2 cup plus 1 tablespoon fresh lemon juice

12 ounces reposado tequila (1 1/2 cups)

Ice

1. In a small saucepan, cook the cranberries and grenadine over medium heat, stirring gently and occasionally, until all the cranberries are soft and just starting to pop, 3 to 4 minutes (you don't want them to turn mushy or break down—they should be soft but intact enough that they can be stuffed into a lychee). Transfer the mixture to a medium bowl and set aside to cool for 10 minutes.

2. Place the lychees in an ice cube tray (1 lychee per compartment) with the hole facing up. Stuff each lychee with 2 softened cranberries, spoon any liquid left in the saucepan over the lychees, and freeze until the lychees are completely frozen, at least 6 hours and up to overnight.

3. Make the simple syrup: In a small saucepan, combine the sugar and water and bring to a simmer over medium heat. Cook, stirring occasionally, until the sugar has completely dissolved, 4 to 5 minutes. Remove from the heat, let cool completely, then transfer to an airtight container and refrigerate until you are ready to make the drinks.

4. To make each martini, in a cocktail shaker, combine 1 1/2 tablespoons (3/4 ounce) each of the lemon juice and simple syrup and 1/4 cup (2 ounces) of the tequila. Add ice, cover, and shake vigorously until cold, about 1 minute. Strain into a martini or coupe glass and add 1 to 2 frozen lychees. Drizzle with grenadine and serve. As the drink changes temperature, the lychees will leak, adding flavor, color, and horror!

MAKES 6 DRINKS

PREP TIME
5 minutes

ACTIVE TIME
15 minutes

TOTAL TIME
6 hours 30 minutes
(includes freezing time)

EASY

◆

Spoon **grenadine** on top of the "eyeballs" to really project the look of **leaking blood**. The bigger the martini glass, the better the effect.

HALLOWEEN MOCKTAILS
WITH BLOODY EYEBALLS

Follow steps 1 and 2 above. Pour 1/2 cup lemon soda and 1/2 cup club soda into each of six glasses. Top each with 1 tablespoon pineapple juice and garnish with 1 or 2 frozen lychees. Drizzle with grenadine and serve immediately.

MINI PORK DUMPLINGS

WITH CHILE DIPPING SAUCE

(Mini Brains)

These dumplings are an unlikely make-ahead wonder! The sauce can be refrigerated for up to three days, and uncooked dumplings can be frozen in a single layer on a parchment-lined baking sheet until solid, then transferred to an airtight container and frozen for up to one month.

FOR THE SAUCE
1/4 cup toasted sesame oil

3 tablespoons Asian chile-garlic sauce

3 tablespoons low-sodium soy sauce

3 tablespoons Chinese black vinegar or rice vinegar

2 tablespoons mirin (Chinese rice wine) or sweet sherry

FOR THE DUMPLINGS
2 tablespoons vegetable oil, plus more for brushing

5 ounces shiitake mushrooms, stemmed, caps thinly sliced

4 large scallions, white and light green parts only, finely chopped

8 ounces baby bok choy, finely chopped (about 1²/₃ cups)

1 small carrot, coarsely grated

3 garlic cloves, finely minced

1 (1¹/₂- to 2-inch) piece fresh ginger, peeled and finely grated (about 4 teaspoons)

3 tablespoons low-sodium soy sauce

1¹/₂ teaspoons mirin (Chinese rice wine) or sweet sherry

1. Make the sauce: In a large bowl, whisk together the sesame oil, chile-garlic sauce, soy sauce, vinegar, and mirin. Cover with plastic wrap and set aside (the sauce will become redder and more ghoulish as it sits).

2. Make the dumplings: In a large skillet, heat the vegetable oil over high heat until shimmering, about 30 seconds; add the mushrooms, scallions, bok choy, and carrot and cook, stirring occasionally, until tender, about 5 minutes. Add the garlic, ginger, soy sauce, mirin, and chile-garlic sauce and cook until the liquid has evaporated, about 3 minutes. Season with salt (you won't need much because of the soy sauce). Transfer the vegetables to a bowl and refrigerate for at least 30 minutes or up to 2 days.

3. Line a large baking sheet with parchment paper. Set a small bowl of water next to your work station.

4. Remove the bowl of vegetables from the refrigerator and stir in the pork until incorporated. Place 3 wonton wrappers on a cutting board and brush the edges with water. Spoon a scant tablespoon of the filling onto the center of each wrapper. Fold the wrapper over the filling and press the edges to seal, pressing the dumpling wrapper directly against the filling and pressing out any air pockets as you go. Use scissors to trim the wrappers, leaving a 1/4-inch border around the filling. Transfer the dumplings to the prepared baking sheet, cover with a damp paper towel, and repeat with the remaining dumpling wrappers and filling (they don't have to look perfect—you are making brains).

MAKES 50 DUMPLINGS

PREP TIME
1 hour 30 minutes

ACTIVE TIME
2 hours

TOTAL TIME
2 hours 15 minutes
(includes chilling time)

INVOLVED

Using a **beaker** really makes these look like **shrunken brains**! Chile-garlic sauce scarily looks like blood, but add **red food coloring** for extra effect. Don't worry about perfect folds in these; rustic looks brainier anyway!

1 teaspoon Asian chile-garlic sauce

Kosher salt

2/3 pound ground pork

50 round wonton wrappers

SPECIAL EQUIPMENT
two-tiered bamboo steamer, wok

5. Line both tiers of a two-tiered bamboo steamer with parchment paper cut to fit and brush the parchment with vegetable oil. Fill a wok or a large skillet with 2 inches of water and bring the water to a boil. Fill the tiers of the steamer with dumplings, making sure the edges don't touch (otherwise, they could stick together). Cover the steamer, place it in the wok, and steam the dumplings until the filling feels firm, about 6 minutes (you can sacrifice one to make sure it's cooked through). Transfer the cooked dumplings to the bowl with the sauce while you steam the remaining dumplings.

6. Carefully use a spoon to completely coat the dumplings with the sauce, then use a slotted spoon to transfer the dumplings to a serving platter. Serve the remaining sauce on the side in a beaker.

ROASTED BEET SOUP

WITH CRÈME FRAÎCHE

(Spider Blood Soup)

¾ cup olive oil, plus more for brushing the bread

1 cup unsweetened pomegranate juice

1 dried bay leaf, broken in half

2 sprigs thyme

Kosher salt and freshly ground black pepper

1½ pounds red beets, greens removed, peeled and cut into ¾-inch chunks (about 4 cups)

1 large red onion, diced

2 garlic cloves, minced

1 tablespoon grated fresh ginger

Sugar

Black sea salt

3 to 6 large slices dark pumpernickel or rye bread (to make 1 bread spider for every bowl of soup)

½ cup crème fraîche

SPECIAL EQUIPMENT
1¾-inch spider-shaped cookie cutter, small squeeze bottle

---

1. Preheat the oven to 375°F.

2. In a 2-quart baking dish, combine 2 tablespoons of the olive oil, the pomegranate juice, bay leaf halves, thyme, and a large pinch each of salt and pepper. Add the beets and stir to coat. Cover with aluminum foil and bake until the beets are very tender (a fork should slide into the beets with no resistance), about 1 hour, stirring once after 30 minutes. Uncover, remove and discard the bay leaf halves and thyme, and set aside. Keep the oven on.

3. In a large saucepan, heat 2 tablespoons of the olive oil over medium heat. When the oil is shimmering, about 1 minute, add the onion, a pinch of salt, and a splash of water and cook until the onion is soft, 6 to 8 minutes. Stir in the garlic and ginger and cook until they soften, about 2 minutes, then pour in 3½ cups water and the cooked beet mixture (with any juices from the pan). Increase the heat to high and bring the liquid to a boil. Reduce the heat to medium-low and simmer until the flavors come together, about 15 minutes.

4. Carefully transfer the beet mixture to a blender, working in batches if necessary. Let cool, uncovered, for 10 minutes, then blend until smooth. With the motor running, remove the small inner cap on the blender lid and slowly drizzle in ¼ cup of the olive oil. Return the soup to the saucepan, taste, and season with sugar, black sea salt, and pepper (the soup should be equally savory, sweet, and tart).

5. Use a 1¾-inch spider-shaped cookie cutter to cut 6 spiders out of the sliced bread, then use a pastry brush to coat both sides of each spider with the remaining olive oil. Season with salt, place on a baking sheet, and toast in the oven until lightly crisp, about 5 minutes.

6. In a small bowl, whisk together the crème fraîche and 1½ teaspoons water, adding additional water if necessary, until the crème fraîche is thin enough to drizzle. Transfer to a small squeeze bottle.

SERVES 4 TO 6

PREP TIME
15 minutes

ACTIVE TIME
40 minutes

TOTAL TIME
2 hours 10 minutes
(includes baking and cooling time),
or 4 hours 10 minutes
if serving soup chilled

EASY

Cut the spider shapes out of the bread **before** toasting it—this prevents tearing!

The wider the bowl, the more cream **"webs"** you can create.

7. The soup can be served warm or cold. To serve warm, heat the soup in a pot over medium-low heat. To serve cold, chill the soup for at least 2 hours.

8. Divide the warm or chilled soup among four to six soup bowls. Squeeze 3 to 5 concentric circles of crème fraîche onto the surface of the soup, then use a butter knife or toothpick to drag lines from the smallest circle through the largest circle to create a spiderweb effect. Top each bowl of soup with a toasted bread spider and serve immediately.

CHARRED BEEF RIB CAGE

WITH BARBECUE SAUCE

(Human Ribs)
15 minutes

---

1 teaspoon whole black peppercorns

½ batch Barbecue Sauce (page 149)

Vegetable oil, for the grill

SPECIAL EQUIPMENT
outdoor grill (optional)

1. Cook the ribs: Place the ribs in a large stockpot. Pour in the cola and add enough water to just cover the ribs. Bring to a boil over high heat, skimming off any foam that rises on the surface. As the liquid is coming to a boil, add the salt and peppercorns. Once the liquid reaches a boil, reduce the heat to low, cover, and gently simmer until the meat is tender but not falling off the bone, about 2 hours. Line a rimmed baking sheet with paper towels. Use a slotted spoon to transfer the ribs to the baking sheet. Discard the cooking liquid; remove the paper towel from under the ribs and discard it.

2. Lightly coat an outdoor grill. Heat the grill to medium-high (or adjust an oven rack 10 inches from the heat source and preheat the broiler to high).

3. Divide the barbecue sauce among three bowls: one for mopping over the raw ribs, one for mopping over the ribs as they cook, and the last bowl for serving alongside the cooked ribs. Working in batches, use a brush to mop the ribs with the barbecue sauce (discard that bowl of barbecue sauce when you're done). Transfer the ribs to the grill and grill until lightly charred on all sides, turning them and brushing with more barbecue sauce as you go, 10 to 12 minutes total. (If using the broiler, put the ribs on a rimmed baking sheet and broil until lightly charred on all sides, turning and brushing the ribs with barbecue sauce as you go, 10 to 12 minutes total.) Transfer the ribs to a platter. Serve with the remaining barbecue sauce alongside.

45 minutes
3 hours

(includes cooking time)

7 to 8 pounds beef back ribs (1 rack), membrane removed and racks cut into individual ribs (about 13 ribs)

2 cups cola

1½ teaspoons kosher salt

To make these ribs look **especially sinister**, take a little extra time to cut away 1 to 2 inches of the meat from around the top of each rib. This exposes more of the **rib bones** and makes it easier for your guests to grab the ribs with their hands.

ROASTED SQUASH SALAD

WITH APPLE CIDER VINAIGRETTE AND SPICY PEPITAS

(Bug Guts)

FOR THE VINAIGRETTE

1 (1-inch) piece fresh ginger, peeled and thinly sliced into rounds

3 cups apple cider or fresh apple juice

Kosher salt and freshly ground black pepper

1 to 3 tablespoons distilled white vinegar

2 tablespoons extra-virgin olive oil

FOR THE SQUASH

1 small acorn squash (about 1½ pounds), halved lengthwise, seeded, and sliced lengthwise along the squash's ridges into wedges

1 small delicata squash (about 12 ounces), sliced into ½-inch-thick rings and seeded

4 tablespoons extra-virgin olive oil

Kosher salt and freshly ground black pepper

FOR THE SPICY PEPITAS

¼ cup hulled raw pepitas (pumpkin seeds)

¼ teaspoon olive oil

Cayenne pepper

Kosher salt

TO ASSEMBLE

5 ounces mixed bitter salad greens (6 cups), such as baby kale, mizuna, and/or baby broccoli leaves

4 ounces hard aged goat cheese, such as Midnight Moon

1. Make the vinaigrette: In a medium saucepan, combine the ginger and apple cider and bring to a boil over high heat, then reduce the heat to medium to maintain a strong simmer and cook until reduced to ½ cup, about 45 minutes. Add a large pinch of salt and stir until dissolved. Let cool completely, then strain through a fine-mesh sieve into a medium bowl. Whisk in 1 tablespoon of the vinegar and the olive oil, then taste and add more vinegar if needed (the dressing should be equal parts sweet and tart) and season with salt and pepper.

2. Meanwhile, roast the squash: Adjust the oven racks to the upper-third and lower-third positions, place a rimmed baking sheet on each rack, and preheat the oven to 425°F.

3. In a large bowl, toss the acorn squash wedges with 2 tablespoons of the olive oil and a large pinch each of salt and pepper. Using an oven mitt, remove the hot baking sheet from the lower oven rack and add the acorn squash in a single layer. Return to the oven on the lower rack. Repeat the process with the delicata squash and the remaining 2 tablespoons olive oil on the other baking sheet. Roast until the bottom of the squash is browned, about 20 minutes, then flip the squash pieces, rotate the baking sheets front to back and top to bottom, and roast until browned on the other side, about 10 minutes for the delicata and about 15 minutes for the acorn squash. Remove the squash from the oven as they're done and let cool completely on the baking sheets. Reduce oven temperature to 350°F.

4. Make the spicy pepitas: Spread the pepitas over a small rimmed baking sheet, toss with the olive oil and a pinch each of cayenne and salt, and toast in the oven until puffed and lightly browned, 7 to 8 minutes; set aside.

5. Assemble the salad: Arrange the salad greens and roasted squash on a large platter. Drizzle with vinaigrette to taste. Use a peeler to shave large strips of the cheese over the greens and squash. Sprinkle with the pepitas and serve. (Any leftover dressing can be stored in an airtight container in the refrigerator for up to 2 weeks.)

SERVES 6 TO 8

PREP TIME
25 minutes

ACTIVE TIME
15 minutes

TOTAL TIME
2 hours 5 minutes
(includes roasting and cooling time)

MODERATE

Place **fake rubber spiders** or cockroaches around the serving platter. Or even better, serve the salad spilling out of a giant rubber spider or cockroaches and call it **"bug gut salad."**

ROASTED APPLE BOMBOLONI

(Doughnut Eyeballs)

FOR THE ROASTED APPLES

1 medium Granny Smith apple (about 6 ounces), peeled, cored, and finely diced or grated

½ tablespoon unsalted butter, melted

1½ teaspoons granulated sugar

⅛ teaspoon ground cinnamon

Pinch of freshly grated nutmeg

FOR THE BOMBOLONI

1 tablespoon honey

½ cup lukewarm water

2 teaspoons active dry yeast

1⅓ cups all-purpose flour, plus more as needed

½ teaspoon kosher salt

4 freeze-dried apple slices (¼ ounce), finely ground in a food processor

1½ tablespoons buttermilk

3 tablespoons granulated sugar

3 large egg yolks

1½ tablespoons unsalted butter, at room temperature

Canola oil

½ cup confectioners' sugar

½ cup of your favorite prepared vanilla pudding

¼ cup of your favorite red fruit jelly or apple butter

SPECIAL EQUIPMENT

deep-fry thermometer, 1½-inch round cookie or biscuit cutter, 2 small squeeze bottles

1. Preheat the oven to 375°F.

2. Make the roasted apples: On a rimmed baking sheet, toss together the apple, butter, sugar, cinnamon, and nutmeg. Bake, stirring every 5 minutes, until the apples are tender, about 15 minutes. Remove from the oven and let cool completely on the baking sheet.

3. Make the bomboloni: In the bowl of a stand mixer, stir together the honey and lukewarm water until combined. Add the yeast and ½ cup of the flour and stir until just combined. Cover the bowl with plastic wrap and set aside at room temperature until the mixture is puffed and bubbling, 45 minutes.

4. Add the remaining flour, the salt, ground freeze-dried apple, buttermilk, granulated sugar, and egg yolks. Stir until just combined, then return the bowl to the mixer and fit the mixer with the dough hook. Mix on low speed until the dough has come together, then add the butter and the cooled roasted apples. Mix on medium speed until the dough is glossy and tacky, about 5 minutes. Scrape the dough into a lightly oiled large bowl, cover with plastic wrap, and refrigerate for at least 8 hours and up to 24 hours.

5. Remove the dough from the refrigerator and let rest at room temperature for 15 minutes.

6. Fill a large Dutch oven halfway with canola oil and affix a deep-fry thermometer to its side. Heat the oil over medium-high heat until it reaches 340°F. Line one rimmed baking sheet with a wire rack and a second with a sheet of parchment paper and keep them nearby.

RECIPE CONTINUES

20 minutes
1 hour 15 minutes
10 hours
35 minutes

(includes chilling time)

Think of these as apple fritters in a **mini-doughnut** form!

Fill these any way you like: whipped cream, apple butter, Nutella...

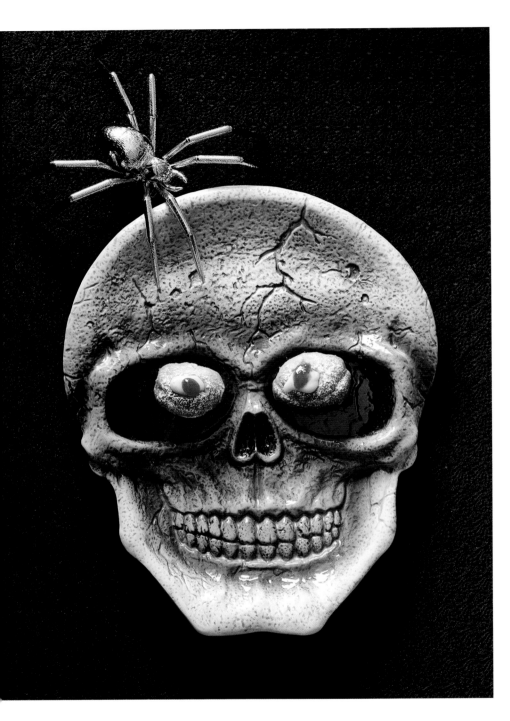

7. While the oil heats, place the confectioners' sugar in a large bowl and some flour in another small bowl. Put the vanilla pudding in a squeeze bottle. Whisk the jelly in a small bowl with just enough water that it is easy to drizzle, then transfer the jelly to the second squeeze bottle.

8. On a floured surface, roll the dough out to a ½-inch-thick round (the dough is fairly sticky, so add extra flour if needed to avoid sticking). Dip a 1½-inch round cookie or biscuit cutter (or inverted shot glass) into the bowl of flour and use it to stamp out about 25 rounds of dough. Squish together the scraps, reroll them, and cut out as many more rounds as you can.

9. Add 10 rounds of dough to the hot oil and fry, using a spider or tongs to flip them as needed so they brown evenly and adjusting the heat under the pot as needed to keep the oil temperature at 340°F, until the bomboloni are browned and just cooked through, 2 to 3 minutes. Transfer to the rack to drain, then roll them in the confectioners' sugar while still warm and arrange them on the parchment-lined baking sheet. Repeat to fry the remaining dough.

10. Use a paring knife to poke a small hole in each bomboloni. Insert the tip of the vanilla pudding–filled squeeze bottle about halfway into a bomboloni and squeeze in the pudding until it starts to come out of the hole; set aside on a serving platter and repeat to fill all the bombolini. Squeeze a small amount of jelly on top of the spot where you can see the pudding. Like all doughnuts, these are best served immediately!

GIVE THANKS FOR LEFTOVERS

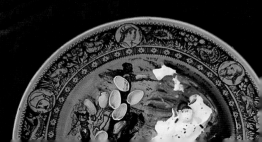

The Friday afternoon or evening after Thanksgiving is the ideal time to host a casual, day-after feast to use up all those leftovers weighing down your fridge. Gather friends and family you didn't see on the first go-round, and out-of-town guests before they head for home. Amp up the cozy factor by eating in the family room with crackling logs burning in the fireplace.

WHAT GUESTS CAN BRING
A favorite leftover dish (but just one, or you'll end up having to have a second leftovers party!). Leftover nuts and party mix for snacking. A favorite football jersey or other gear to support their team while watching the game.

GET GUESTS INVOLVED
Get people to help with the dishes and with putting together the Leftover Pie Sundaes. Guests can get the fire going, pull out extra blankets, and gather warm socks as stand-ins for slippers. Have someone take a poll of football games and movies and create a crowd-pleasing TV-watching schedule with something for everyone.

WHAT TO WEAR
A come-as-you-are wardrobe to enjoy a lazy day off together. Your comfiest clothes with expandable waists—pajamas, sweatpants, and bedhead included!

THE TABLE
Lay down a fresh tablecloth, but use yesterday's Thanksgiving decorations—a bowl of apples, pomegranates—as centerpieces. Relight yesterday's half-burned candles to create a warm glow.

THE FLOWERS
Whatever remains from yesterday, of course!

THE DRINKS
Encourage guests to bring their leftover cider, wine, and beer from the previous day's meal. Serve alongside sparkling water, fresh juice, and coffee.

ACTIVITIES
Lounge by the fireplace. Watch holiday movies. Play board games. Start up a game of touch football.

PARTY BASICS

Anything you can throw together without having to leave the house!

PARTY UPGRADES

Add floor pillows to your family room so everyone has a space to sink into. Hold a sandwich-making competition, with prizes given out for best leftovers combination. Play charades, using Thanksgiving-themed movies as the subject.

OVER-THE-TOP IDEAS

Gift each guest a pair of slippers, and hand out cozy throws for cuddling in front of the fire (bonus points if they can take them home!).

PLAN AHEAD
(OR, IN THIS CASE, DON'T!)
This party's about giving the cook a break, and since everything is so easy, you can ask different guests to work on different recipes. As the day goes on, someone can make the biscuits, the herb cocktail—all hands on deck!

HOST CRAFT PROJECT
Make everyone pumpkin, persimmon, or apple muffins for the next day's breakfast.

PARTY PROJECT
Provide decorative cards and pens so people can write down what they're thankful for as a keepsake of the moment in time, or relay their gratitude to another person in attendance—anonymously or otherwise.

KEEP THE PARTY GOING
Put on a football game. Watch a special movie. Start a wicked game of Monopoly or Risk.

PLAYLIST

"River," Leon Bridges

"Thanksgiving," George Winston

"Home Cookin',"
Jr. Walker and the All Stars

"Come Away with Me,"
Norah Jones

"Thanksgiving Theme,"
Vince Guaraldi

"Bring It on Home to Me,"
Sam Cooke

"Be Thankful," Natalie Cole

"A Song for You,"
Donny Hathaway

"Dream a Little Dream of Me,"
Ella Fitzgerald

"Friends," Bette Midler

"We Are Family," Sister Sledge

"Thankful," Kelly Clarkson

"Home," Michael Bublé

Handwritten notes: "IN @ 2.00", "ANNE BRINGING", "THANKFUL", "DAD :)", "JEN — Has Leftover Pumpkin Pie!"

Leftover Loaded Sweet Potato Skins
Recipe Courtesy of David Burtka

Note—So these sweet potato skins do require a little bit of planning because you have to make sure that you save the skins from your roasted sweet potatoes BUT who doesn't have sweet potatoes somewhere on their Thanksgiving menu? Hopefully you see this recipe before you throw out your skins because this is a much better fate for them rather than in the garbage pail.

The skins from 6 large sweet potatoes that have been roasted, halved length-wise and most of the flesh scooped out (a thin layer of flesh about 1/8-inch thick is ideal), from about 5 1/2 pounds raw sweet potatoes, 12 halves total
3 tablespoons canola oil
Kosher salt and freshly ground black pepper
4 ounces sharp cheddar cheese, shredded, about 1 1/2 cups
8 slices cooked bacon, crumbled, about 3/4 cup
3/4 cup sour cream
2 tablespoons sliced chives

Set 1 rack in the lower third and 1 rack on the upper third of the oven and pre 400 degrees F.

Divide the sweet potatoes between 2 baking sheets and brush on all sides w canola oil and season liberally with salt and pepper. Bake in the oven-side until the edges of the potatoes start to brown, 12-15 minutes. Remove the po the oven and use a pair of tongs to gently flip the potatoes so that they are s Put the potatoes back in the oven, switching the baking sheets top to bottom. the skins are crispy, 12-15 additional minutes.

Remove the potatoes from the oven and use a pair of tongs to gently flip the potatoes so that they are skin-side-down. Sprinkle the cheese and bacon evenly in to the flesh side of the 12 potato halves. Return to the oven and bake until the cheese is just melted, 3-5 minutes. Transfer to a serving platter then top each potato skin with a dollop of sour cream and a sprinkle of chives. Serve immediately.

Yield: 12 potato skins
Prep Time: 15 minutes
Cook Time: 30 minutes
Inactive Prep Time: N/A
Ease of preparation: Easy

Active Time: 45 minutes
Total Time: 45 minutes

Leftover Turkey and Stuffing Dumpling
Recipe Courtesy of David

2 tablespoons canola oil
1 medium yellow onion, 1/2-inch dice,
Kosher salt and freshly ground black p
2 large cloves garlic, minced
2 cups leftover gravy
1 cup leftover mashed potatoes
4 cups low-sodium chicken or turkey stock
1 cup frozen peas
2 cups leftover roasted vegetables
1 pound leftover cooked turkey, cut in to 1/2-inch cubes, about 4 cups
2 large eggs, beaten
6-8 tablespoons all-purpose flour
2 tablespoons roughly chopped flat-leaf parsley
2 cups leftover stuffing
Worcestershire sauce, to taste
White wine vinegar, to taste

Heat the canola oil in a short stock pot over medium heat. Add the onion, a splash of water and a pinch of salt and pepper and cook until the onion is tender and lightly browned, about 8 minutes, stirring occasionally. Add the garlic and cook until softened, about 2 minutes, stirring constantly. Stir in the gravy, mashed potatoes and stock and bring to a boil. Reduce to a simmer and cook, uncovered, for 15 minutes.

Meanwhile, stir the eggs, 6 tablespoons flour and parsley together in a medium bowl. Crumble the stuffing over the mixture and use your hands to mix everything until just combined. If the mixture seems too wet, add 1-2 tablespoons of additional flour. Reserve.

Stir the peas, roasted vegetables and turkey in to the simmering soup. Bring the mixture back to a simmer. The thickness of the stew will depend on the gravy and mashed potatoes you use. It should be thick like a stew, but not too gelatinous. Thin the soup with up to a 1 cup of water, depending on your preference for the consistency of the soup. Take a taste of the soup and add Worcestershire sauce, while wine vinegar and salt and pepper as needed to add flavor and acid (how much you will need of each will depend greatly on the leftovers you use). Drop heaping tablespoons of the stuffing dumpling mixture in to the simmering soup, about 18 total, then cover the pot with a tight-fitting lid. Cook until the dumplings have puffed and are just cooked through, about 10 minutes. Ladle the soup and dumplings in to 6-8 bowls and serve immediately.

Yield: Serves 6-8
Prep Time: 15 minutes
Cook Time 35 minutes
Inactive Prep Time: N/A

Leftover Herb and Celery Mocktail
Recipe Courtesy of David Burtka

3/4 cup granulated sugar
1 small bunch thyme, about 1/2 ounce, plus 8 individual sprigs for garnish
6 large sage leaves
8 celery stalks, about 1 pound, cleaned well
1/4 cup fresh lemon juice
Tonic water, for topping

Stir together the sugar and 3/4 cup water in a small saucepan. Bring to a simmer over medium heat and cook until the sugar completely dissolves, 3 to 5 minutes. Add the thyme bunch and sage leaves. Using a spoon, press down on the herbs to make sure that they are completely submerged. Allow the syrup to cool to room temperature in the saucepan, about 1 hour.

Meanwhile, slice the celery, about 4 heaping cups, and add to a blender along with 1/2 cup plus 2 tablespoons water. Blend until completely smooth then strain through a fine-mesh strainer set over a medium bowl. Use a rubber spatula to stir and push down on the celery pulp to extract as much juice and flavor as possible. You should have a little more than 2 cups of celery juice.

Rinse out the strainer and use it to strain the cooled herb syrup in to a second medium bowl or liquid measuring cup. Use the back of a spoon to press down on the herbs to extract as much flavor as possible.

To make 1 mocktail, add 1 ounce of herb syrup, 3 ounces of celery juice, and a splash of lemon juice (about 2 teaspoons) to a cocktail shaker. Add enough ice to fill the cocktail shaker. Cover tightly and shake vigorously for a few seconds, until the mixture is very cold. Double-strain into a lowball glass filled with crushed ice. Top with a splash of tonic water. Garnish with a thyme sprig and serve immediately. Use the remaining ingredients to make 5 additional mocktails. Keep any leftover herb syrup in a tightly sealed container in the refrigerator.

Yield: Serves 6
Prep Time: 15 minutes
Cook Time: 5 minutes
Inactive Prep Time: 1 hour
Ease of Preparation: Easy

Active Time: 20 minutes
Total Time: 1 hour 20 minutes (includes cooling time)

Leftover Pie Sundaes with Apple Cider Caramel Sau
Recipe Courtesy of David Burtka

Note—This is a great way to use leftover components fro
Extra toasted pecans or walnuts? Add a sprinkle! Leftover
dollop and no one will complain.

1 cinnamon stick
1 1/2 cups apple cider
Kosher salt
1 tablespoon apple cider vinegar
3/4 cup light brown sugar, lightly packed
1/2 cup (1 stick) unsalted butter, cold, cut in to cubes
1/4 cup heavy cream
6 slices of your favorite fruit, pecan and/or pumpkin pie
2 pints vanilla ice cream

Combine the cinnamon stick and apple cider in a small saucepan. Bring to a boil over medium-high heat then reduce to a strong simmer and cook until reduced to 1/4 cup, about 25 minutes. Remove the cinnamon stick then add 1/2 teaspoon salt, vinegar, brown sugar, butter and cream to the saucepan. Bring to a boil over medium heat, stirring constantly. Cook until the mixture is thickened to the consistency of pancake syrup, about 5 minutes. Transfer to a medium bowl and cool completely at room temperature, stirring occasionally, 1-2 hours. The caramel will thicken as it cools.

To serve, cut the slices of pie in to large chunks and layer a couple pieces in to the bottom of 6 large sundae glasses (or whatever tall glasses you have) followed by a couple scoops of ice cream. Drizzle with spoonfuls of the caramel sauce. Repeat this layering process once more then serve immediately. Refrigerate any extra caramel sauce. It will keep for 2 weeks in a tightly-sealed container and just needs to be warmed up slightly on the stove-top or in the microwave to make it pourable again.

Yield: About 1 1/2 cups
Prep Time: 5 minutes
Cook Time: 30 minutes
Inactive Prep Time: 1-2 hours
Ease of Preparation: Easy

Active Time: 35 minutes
Total Time: 2 hours 35 minutes (includes cooling time)

Leftover Mashed Potato Biscuits with Cranberry Butter
Recipe Courtesy of David Burtka

Leftover Mashed Potato Biscuits:
Kosher salt and freshly ground black pepper
3 tablespoons granulated sugar
1 tablespoon plus 2 teaspoons baking powder
2 3/4 cups all-purpose flour
1/2 cup (1 stick) unsalted butter, frozen
2 cups leftover mashed potatoes
1 large egg, beaten
2/3 cup buttermilk, plus additional for brushing, chilled

Cranberry Butter:
1/2 cup (1 stick) unsalted butter, softened
1/3 cup leftover cranberry sauce

For the Leftover Mashed Potato Biscuits:
Set a rack set in the upper third of the oven and pre-heat to 450 degrees F. Whisk together 1 teaspoon salt (depending on the mashed potatoes you use, add up to an additional 1/2 teaspoon of salt), 1 teaspoon black pepper, sugar, baking powder and flour in a large bowl.

Grate the butter on the large hole of a box grater then add to the flour mixture. Use your hands to rub the butter in to the flour until the mixture resembles coarse crumbs. Add the mashed potatoes and mix with a fork until everything just comes together.

Make a well in the center of the mashed potato mixture and add the beaten egg and buttermilk. Mix with a fork until the mixture resembles a loose dough. Turn out on to a lightly floured surface and knead a few times until the dough just comes together (do not overmix). Pat the dough in to a 9-inch square about 1-inch thick then cut in to 16 square pieces. Place on to a baking sheet lined with parchment paper and brush all over with buttermilk. Bake until the tops are lightly browned, about 15 minutes. Cool for 5 minutes on the baking sheet then serve immediately.

For the Cranberry Butter:
Combine the butter and cranberry sauce in a small food processor and whip until completely blended (a few small bits of cranberry is fine). Transfer to a small bowl and serve immediately.

Yield: 16 biscuits and a scant 1 cup of cranberry butter
Prep Time: 20 minutes
Cook Time: 15 minutes
Inactive Prep Time: 5 minutes
Ease of Preparation: Easy

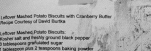

HERB AND CELERY COCKTAIL

What a great way to use up the inevitable leftover herbs from that mega meal prep! When a cocktail both makes you happy and feels healthy, you've got a winner.

¾ cup sugar

1½ cups water

1 small bunch thyme, plus 6 sprigs for garnish

6 large fresh sage leaves

10 celery stalks, thinly sliced

9 ounces gin (1 cup plus 2 tablespoons)

¼ cup fresh lemon juice

Ice

Tonic water

LEFTOVER HERB AND CELERY
MOCKTAIL

Increase the amount of celery to 15 stalks and blend it with 1 cup plus 2 tablespoons water. Make the cocktail as instructed, omitting the gin and increasing the amount of celery juice added to the cocktail shaker to 6 tablespoons.

---

1. In a small saucepan, combine the sugar and ¾ cup of the water and bring to a simmer over medium heat. Cook, stirring occasionally, until the sugar has dissolved, 4 to 5 minutes. Add the thyme bunch and sage leaves, using a spoon to press down on the herbs to make sure they are completely covered by the sugar syrup. Set aside at room temperature for 1 hour to let the flavors infuse.

2. Meanwhile, in a blender, combine the celery and the remaining ¾ cup water and puree until smooth, then strain through a fine-mesh sieve set over a medium bowl, using the back of a spoon or a rubber spatula to push down on the celery pulp to extract as much juice as possible (you should end up with about 1½ cups celery juice). (The celery juice can be made the day before and stored in an airtight container in the fridge until ready to use.)

3. Rinse the strainer, set it over a second medium bowl, and strain the cooled herb syrup, using the back of a spoon or rubber spatula to press down on the herbs to extract as much syrup as possible. Discard the herbs.

4. To assemble each cocktail, in a cocktail shaker, combine 2 tablespoons (1 ounce) of the herb syrup, 1½ ounces of the gin, ¼ cup (2 ounces) of the celery juice, and 2 teaspoons of the lemon juice. Add enough ice to fill the cocktail shaker (about 4 cubes), cover tightly, and shake vigorously for a few seconds, until the mixture is very cold.

5. Hold a mesh strainer over the top of the strainer on the shaker top and double-strain the cocktail into a lowball glass filled with crushed ice. Repeat for each cocktail. Add a splash of tonic water to each glass, garnish with a thyme sprig, and serve immediately. (Any leftover herb syrup can be stored in an airtight container in the refrigerator for up to 1 month.)

15 minutes
15 minutes

1 hour 30 minutes
(includes infusing time)

Most herbs are great for the syrup, but avoid rosemary, which can taste medicinal.

DUMPLING SOUP

2 tablespoons canola oil

1 medium yellow onion, diced

Kosher salt and freshly ground black pepper

2 large garlic cloves, minced

2 cups leftover gravy

1 cup leftover mashed potatoes

4 cups low-sodium chicken stock or turkey stock

2 large eggs

6 to 8 tablespoons all-purpose flour

2 tablespoons coarsely chopped fresh flat-leaf parsley

2 cups leftover stuffing

2 cups leftover roasted vegetables

1 pound leftover cooked turkey, shredded (4 cups)

Worcestershire sauce

White wine vinegar

1 cup frozen peas

> Don't worry if you don't have these exact ingredients— use what you have!

1. In a large soup pot, heat the canola oil over medium heat. Add the onion, a splash of water, and a pinch each of salt and pepper and cook, stirring often, until the onion is lightly browned, about 8 minutes. Add the garlic and cook, stirring, until fragrant and soft, about 2 minutes. Stir in the gravy, mashed potatoes, and stock and bring to a boil. Reduce the heat to medium-low and simmer until slightly thickened, about 15 minutes.

2. Meanwhile, in a medium bowl, whisk together the eggs, 6 tablespoons of the flour, the parsley, and a pinch of salt. Crumble the stuffing over the mixture and use your hands to mix everything until just combined. If the mixture is too wet, add 1 to 2 tablespoons more flour.

3. Stir the roasted vegetables and turkey into the soup and return it to a simmer. The thickness of the soup depends on the gravy and mashed potatoes you use; if it's too thick, thin it with water, 1 cup at a time, until it has a nice consistency. Taste as you go, adding a few dashes of Worcestershire, some vinegar, and salt and pepper as needed.

4. Drop heaping tablespoons of the stuffing mixture into the simmering soup (you should have enough for about 18 dumplings). Cover the pot and cook until the dumplings puff and are just cooked through, about 10 minutes, adding the peas during the last 2 minutes. Divide among six to eight bowls and serve.

SERVES 6 TO 8

PREP TIME
15 minutes

ACTIVE TIME
15 minutes

TOTAL TIME
1 hour

MODERATE

These **kitchen-sink** dumplings couldn't be easier! Throw in **other leftovers**, and use up all the food you have!

SWEET POTATO SKINS

I like these better than regular potato skins—they combine sweet and savory flavors so well! These do require a little bit of planning because you have to make sure you save the skins from your roasted sweet potatoes . . . but then again, who doesn't have sweet potatoes somewhere on their Thanksgiving menu? Hopefully you see this recipe before you throw out your skins, because this is a much better fate for them than the garbage pail.

6 large sweet potatoes, roasted and cooled (see box)

3 tablespoons canola oil

Kosher salt and freshly ground black pepper

1½ cups grated sharp cheddar cheese (6 ounces)

8 slices bacon, cooked and crumbled (about ¾ cup)

¾ cup sour cream

2 tablespoons sliced fresh chives

1. Adjust the oven racks to the upper-third and lower-third positions and preheat the oven to 400°F.

2. Halve the roasted sweet potatoes lengthwise and scoop most of the flesh out, leaving a ⅛-inch-thick shell (save the flesh for another use). Divide the sweet potatoes between two rimmed baking sheets. Brush the shells on all sides with the canola oil and generously season with salt and pepper. Turn the shells scooped-side up and bake until the edges start to brown, about 15 minutes. Use tongs to turn the potatoes over, and rotate the baking sheets from top to bottom. Bake until the shells become crispy, 12 to 15 minutes more.

3. Remove the sweet potatoes from the oven and turn them over again so they're scooped-side up. Evenly sprinkle them with the cheese and bacon, then return them to the oven and bake until the cheese just begins to melt, 4 to 5 minutes. Transfer to a platter and serve each topped with a dollop of sour cream and sprinkled with some chives.

MAKES 12 POTATO SKINS

PREP TIME
25 minutes

ACTIVE TIME
20 minutes

TOTAL TIME
1 hour

MODERATE

Save the sweet potato centers for your favorite sweet potato pie, dumpling, or gnocchi recipe.

HOW TO
ROAST SWEET POTATOES

Preheat the oven to 425°F. Scrub the sweet potatoes and stab them with a fork or a knife in several places. Place the potatoes on a baking sheet and roast for about 1 hour, until the potatoes are very soft on the inside and may even be oozing where you punctured the skins. Remove from the oven and let cool.

LEFTOVER MASHED POTATO BISCUITS

WITH CRANBERRY BUTTER

FOR THE BISCUITS

2¾ cups all-purpose flour, plus more for shaping

3 tablespoons sugar

1 tablespoon plus 2 teaspoons baking powder

1 teaspoon kosher salt, or more to taste

1 teaspoon freshly ground black pepper

½ cup (1 stick) unsalted butter, frozen

2 cups leftover mashed potatoes or sweet potatoes

⅔ cup buttermilk, plus more for brushing

1 large egg

FOR THE CRANBERRY BUTTER

½ cup (1 stick) unsalted butter, at room temperature

⅓ cup leftover cranberry sauce

1. Make the biscuits: Adjust an oven rack to the upper third of the oven and preheat the oven to 450°F. Line a rimmed baking sheet with parchment paper.

2. In a large bowl, whisk together the flour, sugar, baking powder, salt (add more or less salt depending on how salty your mashed potatoes are), and pepper.

3. Set a box grater into the dry ingredients and grate the frozen butter on the large holes directly into the flour mixture. Use your fingers to rub the butter into the flour until the mixture resembles coarse crumbs and any butter pieces are no larger than a pea. Add the mashed potatoes and use a fork to mix until they're evenly incorporated and the mixture resembles clumpy wet sand.

4. Make a well in the center of the mashed potato mixture and add the buttermilk and egg. Use the fork to mix until the dough loosely comes together and there aren't any dry spots, but take care not to overmix.

5. Turn the dough out onto a lightly floured surface and knead a few times, just until the dough comes together (do not overmix). Pat the dough into a 9-inch square about 1 inch thick, then cut it into 16 squares. Place the biscuits on the prepared baking sheet at least 2 inches apart and brush them all over with buttermilk. Bake the biscuits until the tops are lightly browned, 15 to 20 minutes. Remove from the oven and let cool on the baking sheet for 5 minutes.

6. While the biscuits cool, make the cranberry butter: In the bowl of a small food processor, combine the butter and cranberry sauce and process until the mixture is completely blended and smooth (a few visible bits of cranberry are okay). Scrape the butter into a small bowl and serve it alongside the warm biscuits.

MAKES 16 BISCUITS
and about 1 cup cranberry butter

PREP TIME
15 minutes

ACTIVE TIME
35 minutes

TOTAL TIME
1 hour 5 minutes

MODERATE

Use extra cranberry sauce in this a-snap-to-make butter. Cranberry sauce is the one thing there is always extra of!

LEFTOVER PIE SUNDAES

WITH APPLE CIDER CARAMEL SAUCE

This is a great way to use leftover components from your Thanksgiving desserts. Extra toasted pecans or walnuts? Add a sprinkle! Leftover whipped cream? Add a dollop and no one will complain. I could eat the tangy, cider-based caramel with a spoon (okay, I *do* eat it that way!).

FOR THE APPLE CIDER CARAMEL SAUCE

1½ cups apple cider

1 cinnamon stick

¾ cup lightly packed light brown sugar

¼ cup heavy cream

1 tablespoon apple cider vinegar

½ teaspoon kosher salt

½ cup (1 stick) cold unsalted butter, cut into small pieces

TO SERVE

6 slices of your favorite leftover pie (apple pie, pecan pie, pumpkin pie, etc.)

2 pints vanilla ice cream

1. Make the apple cider caramel sauce: Bring the apple cider and cinnamon stick to a boil in a small saucepan over medium-high heat. Reduce the heat to medium and simmer until the cider is reduced to ¼ cup, about 25 minutes.

2. Remove and discard the cinnamon stick and stir in the brown sugar, cream, vinegar, and salt. Add the butter and bring to a boil over medium heat, stirring constantly. Cook until the mixture is the consistency of pancake syrup, about 5 minutes. Pour into a medium bowl and cool completely at room temperature, stirring occasionally, for at least 1 to 2 hours; the caramel thickens as it cools. Extra caramel sauce keeps in an airtight container in the fridge for up to 2 weeks; reheat in the microwave or in a saucepan before using.

3. Make the sundaes: Cut the pie into large chunks and add a couple of pieces to the bottom of six large sundae glasses (or whatever tall glasses you have), followed by a couple of scoops of ice cream. Drizzle with a few spoonfuls of the caramel sauce. Repeat this layering process once more and serve immediately.

SERVES 6 TO 8

makes 1½ cups caramel sauce

PREP TIME
5 minutes

ACTIVE TIME
15 minutes

TOTAL TIME
1 hour 50 minutes
(includes cooling time)

MODERATE

Any leftover pie works here, especially with an assist from a pint of vanilla ice cream.

SNOW DAY

Snow Day Playlist

Let it snow
Fox in the snow
Hazy shade of winter
Sweater weather
Snowbird
Snow
White Winter Hymn
Cold Weather
Cold Rain and Snow
Stormy Weather
Winter Song

Let a snow day bring everyone together to cook and enjoy the warmth of your home. Invite anyone who's off from school or snowed in by the bad weather; it's the perfect excuse to not leave the comfort of your kitchen—or to make the snowy trek over to a neighbor's house that's within walking distance.

When I was growing up in the Midwest, there were months where every day was a snow day, whether we got to stay home from school or not. There were acres of rolling hills and trails right behind our house, and my sister, friends, and I would spend hours happily skating on the pond, sledding a little too fast for our own good, and having epic snowball fights.

WHAT GUESTS CAN BRING
Hot chocolate, board games, DVDs, flavored syrups for fresh-snow snow cones.

GET GUESTS INVOLVED
Ask friends to customize snow cone flavors, grate the cheese, make the onion dip, and build a fire. They can also help set the table, organize the games, and set up the coffee and hot cocoa.

WHAT TO WEAR
Pajamas, big soft sweaters, slippers, cozy hats.

THE TABLE
Cover with a snow-fabric blanket, battery-powered LED twinkle lights, a draping icicle tablecloth, white plates, and napkins with silver accents.

THE FLOWERS
Evergreens gathered from outside, birch branches, homemade paper and white silk flowers, white roses and carnations—basically, anything white and glittery. Collect vintage thermoses and use them as vases for the flowers.

THE DRINKS
A hot cocoa bar, hot cider, hot toddies, coffee, and tea.

PLAN AHEAD
Since snow days usually come on with little advance notice, there's not much work you can do beforehand. But you can certainly get the table set, make the chips one day in advance, and make the dip and the pie.

HOST CRAFT PROJECT
Make your own snow by combining two 16-ounce boxes cornstarch, 1 to 2 cans shaving cream, and glitter of your choice in a giant vessel of some kind (kiddie pool, barrel, giant galvanized metal tub, etc.)!

PARTY BASICS

Read *The Snowy Day* by Ezra Jack Keats; make a snowman kit.

PARTY UPGRADES

Make dye for snow art; play snow-day bingo. Provide snow-cone kits and fake snow crafts.

OVER-THE-TOP IDEAS

Bring in some winter party photo props; buy a snowblower to add some excitement. Make handmade icicles by cutting white paper into icicle shapes or shaping cotton wool and hanging it from different surfaces in the house.

ACTIVITIES

Make maple syrup candy, build a snowman, have a snowball target competition or a human Iditarod race.

PARTY PROJECT

Ask everyone to bring one accessory for decorating the ultimate themed snowman. Think of a theme—drag snowman, Little Red Riding Hood—you get the picture!

GIFTS FOR GUESTS

Goodie bags, a copy of *The Snowy Day*, snow globe kits, hot cocoa mix, seasonal cookies.

KEEP THE PARTY GOING

Make snow-art materials by combining powdered tempera paint and water in spray bottles, or mixing food coloring with water in squeeze bottles. Kids of all ages can then go outside and decorate the snow.

PLAYLIST

"Let It Snow," Diana Krall

"Through the Storm,"
Aretha Franklin and Elton John

"Fox in the Snow,"
Belle and Sebastian

"A Hazy Shade of Winter,"
Simon and Garfunkel

"Sweater Weather,"
The Neighbourhood

"Snowbird," Elvis Presley

"Snow (Hey Oh),"
Red Hot Chili Peppers

"White Winter Hymnal,"
Fleet Foxes

"Bad Weather," The Supremes

"Cold Rain and Snow,"
Grateful Dead

"Stormy Weather," Etta James

"Winter Song," Sara Bareilles
and Ingrid Michaelson

"Baby, It's Cold Outside,"
Ella Fitzgerald and Louis Jordan

Have fun with the hot cocoa bar—think powdered sugar doughnut holes to look like snowballs and mini candy canes to hang from the edge of mugs.

SPICY SWEET POTATO CHIPS

WITH CARAMELIZED ONION DIP

6 tablespoons (¾ stick) unsalted butter

8 sprigs thyme

2 large yellow onions, halved and thinly sliced (about 3 cups)

Kosher salt and freshly ground black pepper

1 cup sour cream

1 (8-ounce) package cream cheese, at room temperature

2 tablespoons fresh lemon juice

Canola oil, for frying

4 small (6-inch-long) sweet potatoes (about 2 pounds)

Cayenne pepper

1 tablespoon thinly sliced fresh chives

SPECIAL EQUIPMENT
deep-fry thermometer, mandoline

1. In a large skillet, melt the butter over medium heat. Add the thyme and cook until the butter starts to brown, 3 to 4 minutes. Remove and discard the thyme, then add the onions and a large pinch each of salt and pepper. Cook, stirring occasionally, until the onions are tender and brown in spots, about 20 minutes. Reduce the heat to medium-low, add a splash of water, and cook, stirring often, until the onions are completely softened and deeply caramelized, about 25 minutes more (if at any time the onions start to stick to the bottom of the pan, stir in another splash of water). Let cool in the pan for 15 minutes.

2. Transfer the onions to a food processor and add the sour cream and cream cheese. Process until smooth, then add the lemon juice and pulse until combined. Taste and season with salt and pepper. Transfer the dip to a serving dish, cover with plastic wrap, and refrigerate while you make the sweet potato chips. (The dip can be stored in an airtight container in the refrigerator for up to 1 week.)

3. Fill a large Dutch oven halfway with canola oil. Heat the oil over medium-high heat until it reaches 350°F. Line a rimmed baking sheet with a wire rack and set it nearby.

4. Meanwhile, use a mandoline to cut the sweet potatoes lengthwise into ¹⁄₁₆-inch-thick slices. Fry the potatoes in the hot oil in batches of 10 to 12 slices at a time, using a slotted spoon to turn them occasionally, until they are browned in spots and crispy, 2 to 3 minutes. Transfer the chips to the rack to drain and immediately season with salt and as much or as little cayenne pepper as you like. Repeat with the remaining sweet potato slices. (The chips can be made a day ahead and stored in an airtight container.)

5. Sprinkle the chives over the dip and serve it alongside the chips.

SERVES 6 TO 8
—
makes about 3 cups dip

PREP TIME
15 minutes

ACTIVE TIME
25 minutes

TOTAL TIME
1 hour 40 minutes

MODERATE

A soup mix works fine, but this is a healthy (and tasty!) alternative.

Feel free to use **store-bought** sweet potato chips, which work just as well.

SLAW

2 medium blood oranges or Cara Cara oranges (about 12 ounces)

½ small head red cabbage, cored and thinly sliced (about 4 cups)

2 small heads frisée (about 6 ounces)

2 scallions, thinly sliced on an angle

¾ cup pomegranate seeds

¼ cup pomegranate molasses

¼ cup red wine vinegar

1 tablespoon whole-grain mustard

Kosher salt and freshly ground black pepper

½ cup extra-virgin olive oil

1. Cut the tops and bottoms off the oranges so they sit flat on a cutting board. Cut away the peel and pith so the flesh is just exposed, then cut the oranges into ¼-inch-thick rounds. Transfer to a large plate and set aside.

2. Place the cabbage in a large bowl. Use a pair of kitchen shears to cut the frisée into 1-inch pieces directly over the bowl. Add half the scallions and half the pomegranate seeds and set aside.

3. In a medium bowl, whisk together the pomegranate molasses, vinegar, mustard, and a large pinch each of salt and pepper. While whisking, slowly stream in the olive oil and whisk until the mixture is creamy and emulsified. Taste and season with additional salt and pepper as needed.

4. Pour half the dressing over the vegetables and toss. Taste and season with salt, pepper, and additional dressing. Arrange three-quarters of the slaw mixture on a large platter and arrange half the orange slices over the slaw. Top with the remaining slaw and orange slices, then sprinkle with the remaining scallions and pomegranate seeds and serve (extra dressing can be stored in an airtight container in the fridge for up to a week).

SERVES 6 TO 8

PREP TIME
15 minutes

ACTIVE TIME
20 minutes

TOTAL TIME
35 minutes

EASY

◆

This is the perfect **make-ahead** salad. It holds up really well due to the frisée and crunchy cabbage. Just make it in advance, refrigerate, and toss with the dressing before serving.

◆

Try swapping out the blood oranges for **navel oranges** or even grapefruit.

THYME AND GRUYÈRE
POPOVERS

5 tablespoons unsalted butter, plus more for serving (optional)

2 tablespoons fresh thyme leaves

¾ cup (3 ounces) finely grated Gruyère cheese

4 large eggs, at room temperature

1½ cups whole milk, at room temperature

1½ teaspoons kosher salt

1½ cups all-purpose flour

Pinch of freshly grated nutmeg

Honey, for serving (optional)

SPECIAL EQUIPMENT
12-cup mini-popover pan (about 3 ounces per cup)

1. Preheat the oven to 450°F. Once the oven comes to temperature, place a 12-cup mini-popover pan in the oven to preheat.

2. In a small saucepan, melt 3 tablespoons of the butter over medium-low heat; remove from the heat and let cool slightly. Cut the remaining 2 tablespoons butter into 12 small pieces and set aside.

3. Combine the thyme leaves and Gruyère in a small bowl and set aside.

4. In a blender, combine the eggs, milk, and salt and blend on medium-high speed until smooth, then add the flour and nutmeg and blend until just combined, 2 to 3 seconds. Pour in the melted butter and blend until the mixture is nice and frothy, about 15 seconds.

5. Using an oven mitt, remove the hot popover pan from the oven and put 1 piece of butter in each cup. Working quickly, divide the batter evenly among the 12 cups, then sprinkle evenly with the thyme and Gruyère. Bake, without opening the oven door, until the popovers are puffed and browned on top, about 20 minutes. Still without opening the oven door, reduce the oven temperature to 350°F and bake until the popovers are deep golden brown, 10 to 12 minutes more.

6. Remove the pan from the oven. Use a small offset spatula to lift the popovers from the pan and a paring knife to poke a small hole in the underside of each to release any steam (this will help the popovers hold their shape). Serve immediately with honey or melted butter, if desired.

MAKES 12 POPOVERS

PREP TIME
10 minutes

ACTIVE TIME
15 minutes

TOTAL TIME
50 minutes

MODERATE

These are so, so easy, but they look so **impressive**. You can even make the batter in the blender the **night before**. Just make sure that right when the popovers come out of the oven, you poke them to help them hold their shape.

A muffin tin will work, but a **popover tin** makes these extra **beautiful**.

POT ROAST AND SAVORY VEGETABLES

3 sprigs rosemary

8 sprigs thyme

1 (3-pound) boneless beef chuck roast, cut into 6 equal pieces

Kosher salt and freshly ground black pepper

2 tablespoons canola oil

4 tablespoons (½ stick) unsalted butter

10 ounces medium cremini mushrooms, stemmed and quartered

2 medium red onions, quartered and cut into 1-inch pieces

3 large carrots, halved lengthwise and cut on an angle into ½-inch pieces

3 celery stalks, cut on an angle into 1-inch pieces

2 large parsnips, peeled, halved lengthwise, and cut on an angle into ½-inch pieces

4 large garlic cloves, thinly sliced

1 (6-ounce) can tomato paste

2 dried bay leaves, broken in half

1½ cups dry red wine

3 cups store-bought mushroom broth

2 tablespoons chopped fresh flat-leaf parsley, for serving

SPECIAL EQUIPMENT
kitchen twine

1. Preheat the oven to 350°F.

2. Tie the rosemary and thyme together with kitchen twine and set aside. Season the meat with 1½ teaspoons salt and ¾ teaspoon pepper. In a large Dutch oven, heat the canola oil over medium-high heat until the oil starts to shimmer, about 30 seconds. Add the meat and sear until deeply browned on both sides, about 5 minutes per side. Transfer the meat to a large plate.

3. Reduce the heat under the pan slightly and add the butter. Once the butter has melted, add the mushrooms and onions (do not add salt at this point, or they will release too much liquid) and cook, stirring occasionally, until the onions are just tender, 8 to 9 minutes. Add the carrots, celery, parsnips, garlic, and a large pinch each of salt and pepper and cook, stirring occasionally, until the vegetables are lightly browned, 6 to 7 minutes. Stir in the tomato paste and cook, stirring frequently, until it darkens slightly, 3 to 4 minutes. Add the herb bundle, bay leaves, and wine and cook, stirring occasionally, until the liquid has reduced and resembles a thick gravy, 4 to 5 minutes. Stir in the broth; increase the heat to high to bring the mixture to a simmer and cook until slightly reduced. Season with salt and pepper. Arrange the meat in the mushroom broth and pour any of the juices left on the plate over the meat. Cover, transfer to the oven, and bake until the meat is fork-tender, about 2 hours.

4. Remove the pot from the oven and set aside for 10 minutes. Discard the herb bundle and bay leaves, then divide the vegetables and cooking liquid among six bowls and top each with some of the cooked meat. Sprinkle with the parsley before serving.

SERVES 6

PREP TIME
20 minutes

ACTIVE TIME
40 minutes

TOTAL TIME
3 hours 10 minutes

EASY

When you dip into a bowl of this, it's total and utter **warm comfort on a spoon**; think family, home, and cozy nights!

Try swapping in other **root vegetables** like celery root, sweet potatoes, and beets to **change things up**.

PEANUT BUTTER PIE

WITH CRUNCHY CHOCOLATE BARK

½ cup (1 stick) unsalted butter, plus more for greasing

1 (9-ounce) package chocolate wafers (about 47 wafers)

Kosher salt

2 cups chilled heavy cream

¾ cup plus 2 tablespoons confectioners' sugar

1 cup cold mascarpone cheese (8 ounces)

¾ cup smooth peanut butter, at room temperature

½ cup cold whole milk

1 cup roasted salted peanuts, coarsely chopped

2 tablespoons unsweetened Dutch-process cocoa powder

1 cup milk chocolate chips (6 ounces)

1. Set a rack in the center of the oven and preheat the oven to 350°F. Butter a 9-inch pie plate.

2. In a medium skillet, melt the butter over medium heat. Cook the melted butter, swirling the pan occasionally, until it starts to bubble and foam, about 2 minutes. Cook, stirring continuously, until the foam subsides and brown flecks start to appear, about 2 minutes more. Transfer to a medium bowl to cool.

3. In a food processor, combine the chocolate wafer cookies and a pinch of salt and pulse until the cookies are broken up, 4 or 5 pulses. Add the browned butter and pulse until the mixture is finely ground and has the texture of wet sand. Press the mixture evenly into the prepared pie plate, making sure the crust goes up all sides of the pie plate. Bake until the crust is mostly dry to the touch and smells fragrant, about 15 minutes, rotating the pie plate halfway through the baking time. Remove from the oven and let the crust cool completely.

4. In the bowl of a stand mixer fitted with the whisk attachment (or in a large bowl using a handheld mixer), beat 1½ cups of the heavy cream on medium speed until the cream forms stiff peaks, about 5 minutes, then transfer to a medium bowl. Sift ¾ cup of the confectioners' sugar into the mixer bowl and add the mascarpone and peanut butter. Beat on low speed until the sugar is incorporated, then add the milk and beat until just combined. Increase the speed to medium-high and beat until completely smooth and creamy, 2 to 3 minutes.

5. Remove the bowl from the stand mixer and use a rubber spatula to gently fold the whipped cream into the peanut butter mixture until completely incorporated.

6. Sprinkle half the chopped peanuts over the bottom of the cooled crust, then top with the peanut butter mixture, making sure to spread the filling to the edges of the crust. Place a piece of plastic wrap directly on top of the pie and refrigerate until completely set, at least 6 hours and up to 1 day.

SERVES 8 TO 12

PREP TIME
20 minutes

ACTIVE TIME
35 minutes

TOTAL TIME
6 hours 35 minutes minimum
(includes chilling time)

EASY

This pie is so **light and dreamy** that when we shot this recipe, the photo shoot crew ate the **whole pie**. Oh, crap! We had to quickly make a duplicate, but no one complained. Ha!

7. In a medium bowl, whisk together the remaining ½ cup heavy cream, the remaining 2 tablespoons confectioners' sugar, and the cocoa powder until the sugar and cocoa powder have completely dissolved. Cover with plastic wrap and refrigerate along with the pie.

8. Line a 13 by 18-inch baking sheet with a silicone baking mat or parchment paper. Put the milk chocolate chips in a heatproof medium glass bowl and microwave in 15-second intervals, stirring with a rubber spatula after each, until completely melted. Transfer the melted chocolate to the prepared baking sheet and spread it into an even layer about ⅟₁₆ inch thick. Sprinkle evenly with the remaining chopped peanuts and let cool to room temperature (the chocolate will not be firm at this point), about 15 minutes. Cover loosely with plastic wrap and refrigerate until firm.

9. When ready to assemble, in the bowl of a stand mixer fitted with the whisk attachment (or in a large bowl using a handheld mixer), beat the cocoa-cream mixture on medium speed until medium peaks form.

10. Spread the whipped cocoa cream on top of the pie, leaving a ½-inch border. Break the firm chocolate into large pieces and press it into the whipped cream. Cut into 8 to 12 slices and serve immediately.

NEW YEAR'S

New Year's Eve is one of the most exciting nights of the year. It's a great opportunity to look forward to the promise of what's ahead and reflect on all the good that was packed into the last 365 days—and you get to do it at home! Prepare for the ultimate New Year's Eve celebration while avoiding crazy traffic, overpriced restaurants, and big crowds. A classy fête is just the right amount of over the top to ring in the new year. Invite your best friends and spoil them rotten while you kick off the new year at your house or in a rented space.

WHAT GUESTS CAN BRING
Champagne, balloons, party favors such as noisemakers, fun glasses, hats.

GET GUESTS INVOLVED
Enlist guests to set up the crafting area with disposable tarps or to man the bar. Ask friends to guest-DJ for 30 minutes at a time.

PARTY BASICS

Craft a cool invitation on card stock. Buy metallic pinwheels and fans. Set up a photo booth with an instant camera for festive party fun.

PARTY UPGRADES

Buy manually activated glitter confetti "push pops" to get people in the festive spirit. Make a craft table for the kids with metallic pens, paper, and stickers. Festoon the room with balloons that spell out "Happy New Year!"

OVER-THE-TOP IDEAS

Create a Champagne-glass tower. Send people home with party-favor fortune cookies with personalized messages you ordered in advance.

WHAT TO WEAR
Your finest duds. Go with a theme: Black and White, Gold and Silver, etc.

THE TABLE
Black, white, gold, silver, copper, glitter, metallics. Use the real silver, and crystal—don't be afraid to mix metals. Scatter glitter on the table. Plates with clocks set on top of them and metal chargers below.

THE FLOWERS
Whites and blushes. Gold- or silver-sprayed gardenia leaves as accents. Peonies, roses, and hydrangeas.

THE DRINKS
Champagne. For the roast: a red Burgundy or Pinot Noir; a white Burgundy for the lobster. Red Bull or other caffeinated energy drinks. A tricked-out coffee bar with flavored creamers and spirits or liqueurs for guests who want to spike their coffee.

PLAN AHEAD
- *Three Days Before:* Make and bake the cream puffs for the Caviar and Chive Cream Puffs. After the puffs are cool, store in a zip-top bag in the freezer for up to a week. When you are ready to use them, set out on the counter for at least two hours before filling.
- *Two Days Before:* Make and freeze the ice cubes for the Champagne Punch; make and mold the Baked Alaskas.
- *One Day Before:* Coat the Horseradish, Herb, and Salt–Crusted Standing Rib Roast; prep the lobster tails; wash the kale.

ACTIVITIES
Fill a bowl with new year's resolutions and go around reading them out loud. Or, even better, have everyone come up with two resolutions and one lie. Have people say them out loud and guess which one is the lie. Create your own time capsule: Ask everyone to bring something to add; in ten years, have the same party and dig it up!

PARTY PROJECT
Create confetti balloons by filling empty balloons with glitter via a funnel. Suspend a sheet from the ceiling, add the balloons, and have a balloon drop at midnight. Saber-open a Champagne bottle with a long, sharp knife.

HOST CRAFT PROJECT
GLITTER CHAMPAGNE BOTTLES

For an easy upscale look, glitterize your Champagne bottles. Fill a small cardboard box (one that will fit your bottle) with your favorite glitter, about ¼ inch deep. Spray adhesive glue over the bottom half of the Champagne bottles. Dip and roll the bottle so the glitter covers the bottom. Repeat with one or even two more colors for an ombré look.

PLAYLIST

"What Are You Doing New Year's Eve?" Ella Fitzgerald

"Will 2K," Will Smith

"Let's Start the New Year Right," Bing Crosby

"Raise Your Glass," Pink

"Happy New Year," Judy Garland

"New Year's Day," U2

"This Will Be Our Year," The Zombies

"Let's Get It Started," Black Eyed Peas

"New Year's Resolution," Otis Redding and Carla Thomas

"Happy New Year," ABBA

"My Dear Acquaintance," Regina Spektor

"Auld Lang Syne," Mariah Carey

A Champagne tower is as easy to create as it looks!

GIFTS FOR GUESTS

Send people home with global symbols of good luck for the new year: long noodles, black-eyed peas, or twelve grapes (one for each month of the new year). Make customized hangover-cure packets with Alka-Seltzer, aspirin, a mini bottle of vodka, and a can of Bloody Mary mix (label the drink fixings as "SOS hair-of-the-dog rescue kits").

KEEP THE PARTY GOING

Dance party! Have everyone take turns playing DJ! Pop twelve grapes into your mouth, burn something (in some cultures, it's a symbol of getting rid of the negativity from the previous year), sing "Auld Lang Syne."

CRANBERRY CHAMPAGNE PUNCH

8 large lemons (about 3 pounds)

1 pound frozen cranberries (about 4 cups)

2 cups unsweetened cranberry juice

10 cinnamon sticks

2 star anise pods

1 teaspoon whole cloves (about 28)

2 cups sugar

1 (750-milliliter) bottle vodka (about 3⅓ cups), chilled

1 (750-milliliter) bottle brut Champagne, chilled

Ice

1. Thinly slice one of the lemons and divide the slices between two 16-ounce plastic containers (deli containers that you have hiding in your cupboard would work great here!). Put ½ cup of the frozen cranberries in each container and fill the containers three-quarters of the way with cold water. Cover with tight-fitting lids and freeze until solid, at least 8 hours (this can be done up to a month in advance of serving).

2. In a medium saucepan, combine 2 cups of the frozen cranberries and the cranberry juice. Bring to a boil over medium-high heat, then reduce the heat to maintain a very low simmer. Add the cinnamon sticks, star anise, and cloves and simmer until the cranberries have all popped open, about 10 minutes. Strain the juice mixture through a fine-mesh sieve set over a medium bowl and discard the cranberries and spices. Immediately add the sugar to the hot juice and stir until completely dissolved. Let the cranberry syrup cool completely.

3. Thinly slice one of the lemons and set it aside for the punch, then juice the remaining lemons (you should get about 1½ cups juice).

4. Remove the giant cranberry and lemon ice cubes from the freezer and allow them to sit in their containers at room temperature for 5 minutes (this tempers the ice so it does not crack when it is added to the punch).

5. In a large punch bowl, combine the lemon juice, half the cranberry syrup, the vodka, and the Champagne. Stir in the plain ice cubes, the remaining frozen cranberries, and the reserved lemon slices. Pop the giant cranberry and lemon ice cubes out of their containers and add them to the punch. Sweeten with additional cranberry syrup, if desired. (Any leftover cranberry syrup can be stored in an airtight container in the refrigerator for up to 2 weeks.)

SERVES 16

PREP TIME
15 minutes

ACTIVE TIME
35 minutes

TOTAL TIME
8 hours
35 minutes
(includes freezing time)

EASY

Be careful
with this fun take on a French 75—it **packs a punch** (pun intended).

VIRGIN SPICED

CRANBERRY AND SPARKLING CIDER PUNCH

6 or 7 large lemons

1 pound frozen cranberries (about 4 cups)

2 cups unsweetened cranberry juice

10 cinnamon sticks

2 star anise pods

1 teaspoon whole cloves (about 28)

2 cups sugar

2 cups unflavored seltzer water, chilled

1 (25.4-ounce) bottle sparkling apple cider, chilled

Ice

1. Follow steps 1 and 2 on page 234 to prepare the giant cranberry and lemon ice cubes and the cranberry syrup.

2. Thinly slice one of the lemons and set it aside for the punch. Juice the remaining lemons (you should get about 1 cup juice).

3. Remove the giant cranberry and lemon ice cubes from the freezer and allow them to sit at room temperature in their containers for 5 minutes (this tempers the ice so it does not crack when it is added to the punch).

4. In a large punch bowl, combine the lemon juice, 1 cup of the chilled cranberry syrup, the seltzer water, and the sparkling cider. Stir in the plain ice cubes, the remaining frozen cranberries, and the reserved lemon slices. Carefully pop the giant cranberry and lemon ice cubes out of their containers and add them to the punch. Sweeten with additional cranberry syrup, if desired. (Any leftover cranberry syrup can be stored in an airtight container in the refrigerator for up to 2 weeks.)

SERVES 16

PREP TIME
5 minutes

ACTIVE TIME
30 minutes

TOTAL TIME
8 hours
40 minutes
(includes freezing time)

EASY

HORSERADISH,
HERB, AND SALT–CRUSTED
STANDING RIB ROAST

This recipe makes enough salt crust to cover a 7- to 8-pound roast, but if you have a smaller or larger roast, it's no big deal—just keep in mind that for every 4 pounds of meat, you will need a half-recipe of salt crust.

FOR THE RIB ROAST

¼ cup packed fresh rosemary leaves

2 tablespoons packed fresh thyme leaves

¼ cup whole black peppercorns

8 garlic cloves

½ cup prepared horseradish, drained, liquid reserved

6 large egg whites

8 cups kosher salt

1 (4-bone) standing rib roast (about 7 pounds)

FOR THE CREAMY HORSERADISH SAUCE

1½ cups crème fraîche or sour cream

½ cup prepared horseradish, drained well

1 tablespoon champagne vinegar

Kosher salt and freshly ground black pepper

2 tablespoons thinly sliced fresh chives

1. Make the rib roast: In a food processor, combine the rosemary, thyme, peppercorns, garlic, horseradish, and egg whites and process until the mixture is mostly smooth, about 30 seconds; transfer to a large bowl. Add the salt and use your hands to stir until well combined; if a spoonful of the mixture squeezed in the palm of your hand holds together like wet sand, the mixture is ready. If not, mix in a tablespoon of the reserved horseradish liquid a little at a time until the mixture holds together.

2. Place the rib roast in a large roasting pan, fat-side up. Pat the herb salt evenly all over the top and sides of the roast in a ¼-inch-thick layer, making sure to mound the salt around the base of the roast so it is completely sealed. Cover with aluminum foil or plastic wrap and refrigerate for at least 2 hours and up to overnight.

3. Remove the roast from the refrigerator and let it rest at room temperature for 1 hour. Preheat the oven to 325°F.

4. Cook the roast for 20 minutes per pound for medium-rare (125°F), about 2 hours 20 minutes for a 7-pound roast (the salt crust might crack; that's okay). Remove from the oven and let rest for 30 minutes.

5. Meanwhile, make the creamy horseradish sauce: In a medium bowl, whisk together the crème fraîche, horseradish, vinegar, and a large pinch each of salt and pepper. Stir in the chives and transfer the sauce to a serving bowl.

6. Use a meat mallet or other heavy kitchen tool to break open the salt crust and discard the crust. Cut the meat away from the bones and thinly slice it crosswise and against the grain. Arrange the sliced meat on a serving platter and serve with the horseradish sauce alongside.

SERVES 8

PREP TIME
20 minutes

ACTIVE TIME
25 minutes

TOTAL TIME
6 hours
35 minutes
(includes chilling, roasting, and resting time)

EASY

Once you've got this rib roast covered in salt, it's a **set-it-and-forget-it** kind of recipe.

Don't be afraid if the **salt cracks**; you will still get a **gorgeous roast**.

BUTTER-ROASTED
LOBSTER TAILS

1½ cups (3 sticks) unsalted butter

6 garlic cloves, smashed

15 sprigs thyme

6 large lobster tails (5 to 6 ounces each)

Flaky sea salt, for sprinkling

SPECIAL EQUIPMENT
twelve 8-inch wooden skewers

1. Preheat the oven to 350°F.

2. In a small saucepan, combine the butter, garlic, and thyme and cook over medium heat until the butter has melted, about 5 minutes. Turn off the heat and let cool while you prepare the lobsters.

3. Using a sharp pair of kitchen shears, cut through the top of each lobster tail, starting from the top and cutting toward the back of the tail, stopping at the tip of the fin. Using a knife, split each lobster tail lengthwise into two pieces. Thread one wooden skewer lengthwise through each lobster half (this will prevent the lobsters from curling up while they cook). Divide the lobsters between two large 9 by 13-inch glass baking dishes in a single layer.

4. Strain the butter mixture through a fine-mesh sieve set over a bowl, using the back of a spoon to press down on the garlic and thyme to extract as much flavor as possible; discard the solids. Pour the butter evenly over the lobster tails and bake, using a pastry brush to baste them with the butter every 5 minutes, until the shells are bright red and the meat is opaque, 10 to 12 minutes. Transfer the lobsters to a large cutting board and let cool slightly; strain the butter again into a small bowl. Remove the skewers from the lobster tails, arrange them on a large serving platter, drizzle generously with the butter, and season liberally with salt. Serve any remaining butter on the side.

SERVES 6

PREP TIME
15 minutes

ACTIVE TIME
45 minutes

TOTAL TIME
45 minutes

MODERATE

◆

Don't get intimidated by the thought of serving lobster at home—it's actually so much **easier** than it looks. Cutting the tails and basting is all there is to it. **To make it even easier,** buy the tails **precut**.

KALE SALAD, THREE WAYS

If you are a kale fan, this twist on a basic kale salad is going to be your new jam. Just watch how fast it flies off the table.

1 bunch Tuscan (lacinato or dinosaur) kale (about 12 ounces)

½ cup plus 2 tablespoons extra-virgin olive oil

Kosher salt and freshly ground black pepper

1 garlic clove, very thinly sliced

1 bunch red kale (about 8 ounces), stemmed, leaves torn into large pieces

⅛ teaspoon finely grated lemon zest

2 tablespoons fresh lemon juice

½ small shallot, finely minced

5 ounces baby kale (about 8 cups)

1 (2-ounce) block Pecorino Romano cheese, shaved

½ cup salted toasted Marcona almonds, coarsely chopped

1. Adjust the oven racks to the lower-third and the upper-third positions and preheat the oven to 250°F.

2. Remove and discard the stems from the Tuscan kale, keeping the leaves as whole as possible. Wash the kale and dry it well.

3. In a large bowl, toss the kale with ¼ cup of the olive oil and a large pinch of salt until all the leaves are coated. Divide between two large baking sheets (this might have to be done in two batches, depending on the size of the baking sheets), spreading them in an even layer with no overlap. Bake, rotating the pans halfway through the cooking time, until crispy, 30 to 40 minutes (the cooking time will vary, so start watching them carefully beginning at 30 minutes). Remove from the oven and let cool completely on the baking sheets.

4. In a large skillet, heat 2 tablespoons of the olive oil over medium heat. Add the garlic and cook until the edges are lightly browned, about 1 minute. Add the red kale and cook, stirring frequently, until just wilted, 1 to 2 minutes. Season generously with salt and pepper and set aside.

5. In a large bowl, combine the lemon zest, lemon juice, shallot, and a pinch each of salt and pepper. While whisking, slowly stream in the remaining ¼ cup olive oil and whisk until emulsified; taste and season with salt and pepper. Transfer half the dressing to a small bowl and set aside. Add the baby kale to the dressing remaining in the large bowl and massage the dressing into the kale until the kale darkens and wilts, about 30 seconds; set aside for 5 minutes.

6. Put the sautéed red kale, the dressed baby kale, half the crispy Tuscan kale, half the cheese, and half the almonds in a large bowl and toss lightly to combine. Transfer to a large platter, drizzle with the remaining dressing, then top with the remaining Tuscan kale, cheese, and almonds and serve.

CAMEMBERT

MASHED POTATOES

8 to 10 Yukon Gold potatoes (3 pounds), peeled and cut into 1-inch chunks

Kosher salt

½ cup (1 stick) unsalted butter

1 cup heavy cream

8 ounces Camembert cheese, white outer rind removed

1. Place the potatoes in a soup pot and cover with 2 inches of water. Season the water liberally with salt. (The water should taste like the sea.) Slowly bring the water to a low simmer over medium heat and simmer until the potatoes are fork-tender, 25 to 30 minutes; drain well.

2. In a small saucepan, combine the butter and cream and heat over medium heat until the butter has melted and the cream is hot but not boiling, 3 to 4 minutes.

3. Working in batches, pass the heavy cream and then the cheese through a food mill fitted with the largest die (holes) into a large bowl, then pass the warm potatoes through into the same bowl so it all gets incorporated into the mash.

4. Gently stir the potato mixture until just combined; taste and season with salt. Transfer to a large bowl and serve.

SERVES 6 TO 8

PREP TIME
10 minutes

ACTIVE TIME
50 minutes

TOTAL TIME
50 minutes

EASY

Whirling **Camembert** into classic mashed potatoes makes for a rich taste. Fancy!

CAVIAR AND CHIVE

CREAM PUFFS

4 tablespoons (½ stick) butter

½ cup water

¼ teaspoon kosher salt

½ cup all-purpose flour

3 large eggs, at room temperature

3 tablespoons finely minced fresh chives

Canola oil cooking spray

½ cup plus 2 tablespoons crème fraîche

3½ ounces American sturgeon caviar (a heaping ⅓ cup; available from online outlets such as Petrossian, ROE, and Russ and Daughters)

1. Preheat the oven to 400°F.

2. In a medium saucepan, bring the butter, water, and salt to a strong simmer over medium heat. Reduce the heat to low, add the flour all at once, and stir with a heatproof rubber spatula until a light coating sticks to the bottom and sides of the pan, 3 to 4 minutes. Turn off the heat and let cool for 5 minutes. Add two of the eggs, one at a time, and stir (with gusto!) until completely incorporated and the dough is smooth, then stir the mixture for 15 seconds more until a stiff peak remains standing when you lift the dough with a wooden spoon. Gently stir in 1 tablespoon of the chives.

3. Dab a small dollop of dough on the inner corners of a large baking sheet, then arrange a piece of parchment paper on the baking sheet, pressing down on the corners to affix the paper. Spray a 1-teaspoon measure and an additional smaller spoon with cooking spray, then use the two spoons to scoop leveled teaspoons of the dough onto the prepared baking sheet, spacing them at least ¾ inch apart (you can also pipe the dough onto the baking sheet using a piping bag fitted with a small round tip). Wet your fingers slightly with water and flatten any peaks on the dough.

4. In a small bowl, whisk the remaining egg with a hefty splash of water and brush the tops of the dough with the egg mixture. Bake, without opening the oven door, until puffed to double their size and golden brown, about 20 minutes.

5. Remove the baking sheet from the oven and set it on a wire rack. Let the puffs cool on the baking sheet for 15 minutes.

6. Cut the cooled puffs in half. Spoon a small amount of the crème fraîche onto the bottom half of each puff, then add a small dollop of caviar and a pinch of the remaining chives on top of the cream.

7. Arrange the puffs on a large serving platter and cover the puffs with their tops before serving.

MAKES 40 TO 50 CREAM PUFFS

PREP TIME
20 minutes

ACTIVE TIME
30 minutes

TOTAL TIME
1 hour 5 minutes

EASY

You can always use **paddlefish roe** in place of caviar; it keeps for months in the fridge.

BAKED ALASKAS

FOR THE DARK CHOCOLATE CAKE
Canola oil cooking spray

¾ cup all-purpose flour

¾ cup packed dark brown sugar

¾ cup unsweetened dark cocoa powder, such as black cocoa

1 teaspoon baking soda

½ teaspoon baking powder

½ teaspoon fine salt

1 large egg

½ cup whole milk

¼ cup canola oil

½ cup hot, strong black coffee

2 pints cookies-and-cream ice cream, softened

FOR THE MERINGUE
8 large egg whites, at room temperature

¼ teaspoon cream of tartar

1 vanilla bean, split lengthwise and seeds scraped out

1¼ cups granulated sugar

¾ cup 100-proof (or higher) brandy (optional)

SPECIAL EQUIPMENT
2½-inch round cookie or biscuit cutter, small kitchen torch or matches

1. Make the cake: Preheat the oven to 350°F. Spray a 9 by 13-inch metal cake pan with cooking spray, line it with parchment paper, and spray the paper.

2. In a medium bowl, whisk together the flour, brown sugar, cocoa, baking soda, baking powder, and salt. In a second medium bowl, whisk together the egg, milk, and oil. Gently stir the milk mixture into the dry ingredients until just combined. Add the hot coffee and stir until the batter is completely smooth.

3. Pour the batter into the prepared pan and bake until puffed and a cake tester inserted into the center of the cake comes out clean, about 15 minutes. Remove from the oven and let cool completely on a wire rack. Invert the cake out of the pan onto a large cutting board, countertop, or other clean, flat surface.

4. Use a 2½-inch round cookie or biscuit cutter to cut 12 circles out of the cake and place them on a small baking sheet (save any leftover cake scraps for another use, such as the Sundae Bar on page 139). Use a 2-ounce (¼-cup) scoop to portion leveled mounds of ice cream on top of each cake round. Set the baking sheet in the freezer and freeze until the cake and ice cream are completely frozen, at least 2 hours and up to overnight.

5. Make the meringue: In the bowl of a stand mixer fitted with the whisk attachment (or in a large bowl using a handheld mixer), combine the egg whites, cream of tartar, and scraped vanilla seeds (save the pod for Vanilla Sugar; see page 250). Whip on medium-high speed until the egg whites are foamy, about 2 minutes. Increase the speed to high and gradually add the sugar, then whip until the egg whites hold stiff, glossy peaks and there are no longer granules of sugar in the meringue, 6 to 7 minutes.

RECIPE CONTINUES

SERVES 12

PREP TIME
20 minutes

ACTIVE TIME
45 minutes

TOTAL TIME
5 hours
20 minutes
(includes cooling and freezing time)

INVOLVED

For a big show, pour the alcohol on the cakes, serve them, and have every adult light their own.

You can put the **whole meringue in the freezer** and pull it out the next day; that way everything will be assembled and **ready to go**.

6. Make the baked Alaskas: Place the cake and ice cream rounds on twelve individual heatproof plates. Top each with a large mound of meringue, then use a small offset spatula or spoon to spread the meringue over the ice cream and cake so both are completely covered. Tap the spatula or spoon against the surface of the meringue and lift to make decorative peaks all over the surface. (Now you can freeze them and serve the next day, or proceed to step 7.)

7. At this point, you have two very fun options (and one that's less fun, but gets the job done): You can use a kitchen torch to brown the meringue, or you can spoon 1 tablespoon of 100-proof brandy onto each baked Alaska, then use a lit match to set it ablaze (keep anything flammable—hair, shirtsleeves—secured and out of fire's way!). Alternatively, you can put all 12 of the built baked Alaskas on a large baking sheet and brown them under a very hot broiler in the center of your oven (the timing for this will depend heavily on your broiler). Use a large spatula to transfer the browned baked Alaskas onto individual plates and serve immediately.

FRESH START BRUNCH

Start the new year on a healthy note! A wellness-focused brunch is just the ticket to jump-start a fresh new year. Invite like-minded friends with a desire to eat healthy and work up a sweat on a morning or afternoon in early January at your house, a spa, a park, a rented room, or the gym.

PARTY BASICS

Vegetable centerpieces, spa water, a DVD of your favorite workout to do with friends. Fill out new year's resolution cards and read them out loud to empower people. Lead a group meditation.

PARTY UPGRADES

Craft a workout wheel where people spin to choose their exercise. Watch a documentary on eating healthy (*Hungry for Change, The Magic Pill, Food Matters,* and *That Sugar Film* are all good choices). Use your home printer to create cards or pamphlets with ideas for living a healthier life. Provide yoga stones with messages and make-your-own meditation beads for inspiration.

OVER-THE-TOP IDEAS

Hire a personal trainer or yoga teacher to teach a class, or make it a spa party with do-it-yourself facials, manicures, and pedicures. Give out party favors like reusable water bottles, headbands, and jump ropes. Send invites that look like rolled-up yoga mats.

WHAT GUESTS CAN BRING
A food journal, yoga mats, sweat towels, water bottles, or instructions for their favorite exercise regimen on paper or on their cell phone.

GET GUESTS INVOLVED
Ask someone to arrange the vegetable platter, arrange a healthy fruit bowl, and set up the bar. Friends can set up the workout area and lead a set of exercises.

WHAT TO WEAR
Sweats, yoga pants, exercise clothes.

THE TABLE
Set out a new yoga mat as a tablecloth. Make the table feel extra fresh with lots of green, yellow, and bright blue accents in the tablescape and flower arrangements.

THE FLOWERS
Cabbage roses, artichokes, Brussels sprouts on the stem, bunches of fresh herbs, brightly colored flowers.

THE DRINKS
Different-flavored spa waters, a make-your-own-smoothie bar with all the fixings (yogurt, fruit, protein powder, flaxseed) and a blender.

PLAN AHEAD
- *Three Days Before:* Freeze berries for the smoothies.
- *Two Days Before:* Make the quinoa for the scramble.
- *One Day Before:* Make the dip.

ACTIVITIES
Do a yoga class. Watch a movie on healthy living. Bring in a nutritionist to give a talk.

PARTY PROJECT
Make-Your-Own Mala Beads: Supply guests with everything they'll need to make a strand of mala (meditation) beads: beads, tassels, cording, and scissors. Ask everyone to sit in a circle as they make their mala strings and state an intention for the new year.

GIFTS FOR GUESTS
Yoga towels, insulated water bottles, healthy snack boxes, sport socks, sunscreen, a great fitness hat.

KEEP THE PARTY GOING
Corral the group for an impromptu run around the neighborhood.

PLAYLIST

"Physical," Olivia Newton-John

"I Will Survive," Gloria Gaynor

"Beautiful Day," U2

"Don't Give Up," Peter Gabriel

"Eye of the Tiger," Survivor

"Rise Up," Andra Day

"You Gotta Be," Des'ree

"Ain't No Mountain High Enough," Marvin Gaye and Tammi Terrell

"Everywhere," Fleetwood Mac

"I Won't Give Up," Jason Mraz

"Don't Stop Believin'," Journey

"Don't Be So Hard on Yourself," Jess Glynne

"Push It," Salt-N-Pepa

CUCUMBER-LIME

SPRITZERS

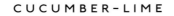

1 large English cucumber, ends removed

½ cup fresh lime juice (from about 4 limes), plus 1 lime, thinly sliced into rounds

3 cups sparkling mineral water, chilled

Ice

Feel free to put **whatever you want** in these—if you want berries or green tea, go for it. Think of these recipes as **templates** to play around with. **Go wild!**

1. Slice 12 thin rounds from the cucumber and set them aside. Coarsely chop the remaining cucumber and transfer it to a blender. Puree the cucumber until smooth, then strain the juice through a fine-mesh sieve set over a medium bowl, using the back of a spoon to press on the pulp to extract as much juice as possible (you should have about 1 cup cucumber juice). Discard the solids.

2. Pour the cucumber juice and the lime juice into a carafe and add the sparkling mineral water.

3. Fill the carafe with ice and stir to combine. Gently stir in the reserved sliced cucumber and lime wheels and serve over ice.

SERVES 6 TO 8

PREP TIME
10 minutes

ACTIVE TIME
10 minutes

TOTAL TIME
20 minutes

EASY

GRAPEFRUIT AND POMEGRANATE

SPRITZERS

2 large Ruby Red grapefruits

½ cup pomegranate seeds, plus more for garnish

3 cups sparkling mineral water, chilled

Ice

1. Thinly slice one of the grapefruits into rounds and set aside. Juice the other grapefruit and pour the juice into a large carafe (you should get about 1 cup juice).

2. Add the pomegranate seeds and sparkling water to the carafe, then fill the carafe with ice. Stir, then add the grapefruit rounds. Serve garnished with more pomegranate seeds.

SERVES 6 TO 8

PREP TIME
5 minutes

ACTIVE TIME
5 minutes

TOTAL TIME
10 minutes

EASY

SPRITZERS

1 (4-inch) piece fresh ginger, peeled and thinly sliced

1 cup boiling water

½ cup honey

½ cup fresh lemon juice, plus 1 lemon, thinly sliced into rounds

3 cups sparkling mineral water, chilled

Ice

1. Put the ginger slices in a large heatproof carafe. Pour in the boiling water and add the honey. Stir until the honey has dissolved. Refrigerate until completely cooled.

2. Add the lemon juice and sparkling water to the carafe, then fill the carafe with ice. Stir to combine, then add the sliced lemon and serve.

SERVES 6 TO 8

PREP TIME
10 minutes

ACTIVE TIME
10 minutes

TOTAL TIME
1 hour 10 minutes
(includes cooling time)

EASY

QUINOA-SPINACH

SCRAMBLE

12 large eggs

⅓ cup whole milk

Kosher salt and freshly ground black pepper

4 tablespoons olive oil

4 cups packed baby spinach (about 4 ounces)

1 cup cooked rainbow quinoa (about 4 ounces)

1 cup of your favorite shredded cheese

1. Crack the eggs into a large bowl; add the milk and a large pinch each of salt and pepper and whisk until well combined; set aside.

2. In a large nonstick skillet, heat 2 tablespoons of the olive oil over medium heat. Add the spinach and a generous pinch each of salt and pepper and cook, stirring occasionally, until just wilted, about 2 minutes. Transfer to a bowl and set aside.

3. In the same pan, heat the remaining 2 tablespoons olive oil over medium heat. Pour in the egg mixture and cook until the eggs are slightly set, about 2 minutes. Use a heatproof spatula to gently stir the eggs (in almost a scraping motion) over low heat until large, soft curds form, 10 to 12 minutes. Be patient with this; perfect soft-scrambled eggs cannot be rushed!

4. When the eggs are mostly, gently stir in the quinoa, cheese, and spinach and cook until the quinoa and spinach are warmed through and the cheese has melted, 1 to 2 minutes. Spoon into a large bowl or onto a large platter.

SERVES 6

PREP TIME
10 minutes

ACTIVE TIME
25 minutes

TOTAL TIME
35 minutes

EASY

◆

The **protein** from the eggs and all the **vitamins** from the spinach will make you feel like you have **superpowers**!

SMOOTHIE

10 ounces mixed frozen berries (about 2 heaping cups)

1 cup plain kefir (drinkable probiotic yogurt; available in the dairy aisle)

1 cup unsweetened plain almond milk

1 heaping tablespoon honey

1. In a blender, combine the frozen berries, kefir, almond milk, and honey and blend on high until smooth.

2. Divide between two glasses and serve immediately.

SERVES 2

PREP TIME
5 minutes

ACTIVE TIME
5 minutes

TOTAL TIME
10 minutes

EASY

This smoothie hides **healthy add-ins** like a champ. For extra punch, feel free to **sneak in greens** like kale or spinach, or probiotics or fiber.

BUTCHER VEGETABLES

WITH CARROT AND BEET DIPS

FOR THE ZESTY BEET AND ALMOND DIP

1/4 cup water

4 tablespoons olive oil, plus more for drizzling

3 tablespoons white wine vinegar, plus more to taste

2 sprigs fresh oregano

3 garlic cloves, lightly crushed

2 medium red beets (about 12 ounces total), peeled and cut into 1-inch chunks

Kosher salt and freshly ground black pepper

1/2 cup slivered almonds

1 (15-ounce) can organic low-sodium brown or black lentils, drained and rinsed well

FOR THE SPICED ROASTED CARROT DIP

1 teaspoon cumin seeds

1 teaspoon coriander seeds

1 teaspoon ground turmeric

Kosher salt

7 medium carrots, cut into 1-inch pieces

1 large shallot, quartered through the root

2 garlic cloves, unpeeled

2 tablespoons refined coconut oil, melted

2 tablespoons fresh lemon juice, plus more to taste

1/4 cup unsweetened plain cashew or almond milk

2 tablespoons water

1. Make the zesty beet and almond dip: Preheat the oven to 375°F.

2. In a 2-quart baking dish, stir together the water, 2 tablespoons of the olive oil, the vinegar, oregano, garlic, beets, and a large pinch each of salt and pepper. Tightly cover the dish with aluminum foil and bake until you can easily pierce the beets with a fork, about 1 hour, stirring once halfway through the cooking time.

3. Meanwhile, spread the almonds over a small baking sheet and toast in the oven until slightly darkened in color and fragrant, 8 to 10 minutes. Remove from the oven and let cool completely.

4. Remove the oregano from the beets and discard. Let the beets and cooking liquid cool slightly, about 15 minutes, then transfer the beets, cooking liquid, and garlic to a food processor. Add the almonds, lentils, the remaining 2 tablespoons olive oil, and a large pinch each of salt and pepper and process until smooth, scraping down the sides of the bowl with a rubber spatula as needed. Taste and season with additional salt, pepper, and vinegar, as needed. Transfer to a small bowl, cover, and chill for 30 minutes, if desired.

5. Make the spiced roasted carrot dip: Preheat the oven to 425°F.

6. Combine the cumin and coriander seeds in a small skillet and toast over medium heat, stirring occasionally, until fragrant, about 3 minutes. Grind in a spice grinder or mortar and pestle until finely ground. Transfer to a small bowl and stir in the turmeric and a large pinch of salt.

7. Spread the carrots, shallot, and garlic over a baking sheet. Add the melted coconut oil, the spice blend, and a large pinch of salt; stir to combine. Roast until the carrots are very tender and browned in spots, about 30 minutes, flipping once halfway through the cooking time. Remove from the oven and let cool slightly.

SERVES 8 TO 12

PREP TIME
25 minutes

ACTIVE TIME
2 hours

TOTAL TIME
2 hours

EASY

I got this idea from a place we went to in **Nice, France**. The tablescape there was filled with an abundance of vegetables and an anchovy aioli, and everyone got **involved**.

TO ASSEMBLE

8 celery stalks, ends trimmed

12 small Tuscan (lacinato or dinosaur) kale leaves

12 whole endive leaves

12 broccolini

8 radishes

4 fennel bulbs

SPECIAL EQUIPMENT

spice grinder or mortar and pestle

8. Peel the garlic cloves and put them in a food processor. Add the carrots, shallots, lemon juice, cashew milk, water, and a large pinch of salt. Process until mostly smooth with a few small carrot chunks still visible, scraping down the sides of the bowl as needed and adding more water by the tablespoonful as needed, about 30 seconds. Taste and season with salt, pepper, and lemon juice. Transfer the dip to a small bowl, cover, and chill for 30 minutes, if desired.

9. Assemble the board: Place the bowls of dip on a large wooden carving board, arrange the vegetables alongside, and place a small paring knife on the board so guests can cut up the vegetables to dip as they wish.

Have people **cut their own vegetables**, and everybody wins!

POACHED SALMON

WITH WINTER GREENS AND PERSIMMON

FOR THE SALMON

1 (750-milliliter) bottle dry white wine (about 3½ cups)

2 tablespoons whole black peppercorns

1 medium orange, sliced into ¼-inch-thick rounds

1 medium lemon, sliced into ¼-inch-thick rounds

2 celery stalks, quartered

2 medium shallots, halved and thinly sliced

4 garlic cloves, lightly smashed

8 flat-leaf parsley stems, leaves reserved

Kosher salt

2½ pounds skin-on center-cut salmon, pin bones removed

FOR THE WINTER GREENS AND PERSIMMONS

¾ cup plus 1 tablespoon extra-virgin olive oil

6 kumquats

1 small shallot, finely minced (¼ cup)

1 teaspoon Dijon mustard

2 tablespoons fresh lemon juice

¼ cup fresh orange juice

¼ cup champagne vinegar

Kosher salt and freshly ground black pepper

4 ounces mixed winter salad greens, such as radicchio, curly endive, and/or tatsoi (10 to 12 lightly packed cups)

2 slightly firm Fuyu persimmons, peeled and sliced into ⅛-inch-thick rounds

SPECIAL EQUIPMENT

instant-read thermometer

1. Make the salmon: In a large roasting pan, combine the wine, peppercorns, orange rounds, lemon rounds, celery, shallots, garlic, and parsley stems. Add enough cold water to come slightly more than halfway up the sides of the pan. Stir in 2 tablespoons salt until dissolved. Taste the liquid and keep adding and stirring in more salt until it tastes well seasoned and pleasantly salty (the salt will season the salmon while it cooks). Set the roasting pan on the stovetop.

2. Add the salmon, skin-side down, and bring the liquid to a very slow simmer over medium heat, 25 to 30 minutes, until an instant-read thermometer inserted into the thickest part of the salmon reads 115°F (if necessary, cook longer and gauge the temperature every few minutes). Use two large spatulas to transfer the salmon to a large platter and immediately season the salmon with more salt; set aside.

3. While the salmon cooks, start the winter greens and persimmons: In a small skillet, heat 1 tablespoon of the olive oil over medium heat. Add the kumquats and fry until caramelized and chewy, 5 to 7 minutes. Set aside.

4. In a medium bowl, whisk together the shallot, mustard, lemon juice, orange juice, vinegar, and a large pinch each of salt and pepper. While whisking, slowly stream in the remaining ¾ cup olive oil and whisk until emulsified. Taste and season with salt.

5. In a separate large bowl, toss the winter salad greens with half the dressing and a pinch of salt. Taste and season with salt and pepper.

6. To serve, top half the salmon with the dressed salad and nestle the sliced persimmons throughout the salad. Scatter the kumquats around and serve. (Extra vinaigrette can be stored in a squeeze bottle or airtight container in the refrigerator for up to 1 month.)

SERVES 8 TO 10

PREP TIME
20 minutes

ACTIVE TIME
10 minutes

TOTAL TIME
1 hour

EASY

Feel free to use **any other greens** here.

This dish can **sit out** on a table or a buffet for a while since the salmon stays so **moist**.

Got leftovers? Put them in the fridge and make a salad with them the next day.

GAME NIGHT

POLISH - AMERICAN CHRISTMAS Carols

Throw a fun, fast-and-loose game night after the holiday break. Invite friends, family, and work colleagues to bring the worst presents they got during the holiday season for a gift swap, and play the white elephant game while you snack on trashy food.

PARTY BASICS

Stockpile consolation prizes for the Worst Gift award. Have other games to play when the take-it-back part is over.

PARTY UPGRADES

Decorate your house in game-night décor—giant dice, menu descriptions spelled out in Scrabble tiles, banners made of strung-together playing cards.

OVER-THE-TOP IDEAS

Make a Candyland-themed candy bar complete with candy canes and gumdrops. Make medals out of candy bars or gift cards.

WHAT GUESTS CAN BRING
Crappy gifts, chips for the dip, games, a running charade list, candy for the candy bar.

GET GUESTS INVOLVED
Have guests put popcorn in bowls, cut up the brownies, and help set the table. Ask someone to write out numbers on a sheet of paper for the white elephant game.

WHAT TO WEAR
Comfy clothes to sit around in—and potentially move around in. As the host, wear bright colors to add a little new year's cheer to cold winter days!

THE TABLE
Use bright and cheery colors. Lay down a Twister mat. (Instead of risers for your food, use game boxes like Scrabble, Trivial Pursuit, and Operation. Use board games for place mats or use Scrabble tiles to spell out what you are serving.

THE FLOWERS
Line the inside of a glass vase with dominos or playing cards. Bright colors: daisies, colored carnations—anything cheery!

THE DRINKS
Leftover beer and wine from all your holiday revelry. Soft drinks and water.

PLAN AHEAD
Make the meatballs and brownies the day before, wrap the gifts, brainstorm prizes, plan backup games, and make the playlist.

HOST CRAFT PROJECT
Make prizes for the winners. For instance, tape blue ribbons on candy bars to make them look like medals.

ACTIVITIES
Play games like running charades, board games, Take It Back, the puzzle game, Celebrity, Pictionary, Cards Against Humanity, Speak Out, and Catch Phrase.

PARTY PROJECT
Have everyone make a running charades list of twenty movies, books, or TV shows that all tie together in some way. Split up into two teams and see who can be the first to act out all the items on the other's list.

GIFTS FOR GUESTS
Send people home with mini gift bags, which could include mini card games, lotto tickets, and movie-size candy boxes.

KEEP THE PARTY GOING
Have everyone choose a "white elephant" song for a dance party.

WHAT'S A WHITE ELEPHANT GAME?

Everyone brings a small gift (either a gag gift or something they're dying to re-gift) and puts it in a pile in the middle of the room. One by one, each guest can either unwrap a gift from the pile or steal a gift that was already opened by a previous guest. (P.S.: A gift can be stolen only three times!)

PLAYLIST

"The Game of Love," Wayne Fontana and the Mindbenders

"Quit Playing Games (with My Heart)," Backstreet Boys

"Poker Face," Lady Gaga

"Game Court," Snoop Dogg

"The Dealer," Stevie Nicks

"Games," Demi Lovato

"Play the Game," Queen

"Queen of Hearts," Juice Newton

"The Joker," Steve Miller Band

"Games People Play," Dolly Parton

"Two of Hearts," Stacey Q

"The Gambler," Kenny Rogers

"Guessing Games," Hall and Oates

SEVEN-LAYER DIP

WITH HOMEMADE TORTILLA CHIPS

2 tablespoons canola oil

2 (4-ounce) cans chopped mild or hot Hatch green chiles, drained

2 (16-ounce) cans refried beans

1 sprig epazote (optional)

Kosher salt and freshly ground black pepper

1 cup sour cream

½ cup mayonnaise

Grated zest of 1 large lime (about 1 teaspoon)

¼ teaspoon ground cumin

2 cups Guacamole (page 62)

8 ounces Monterey Jack cheese, shredded (about 2 cups, or use preshredded cheese)

1 head romaine lettuce, thinly sliced (about 3 cups)

1 (2.25-ounce) can sliced black olives, drained

2 scallions, thinly sliced

2 radishes, thinly sliced

Hot sauce

Homemade Tortilla Chips (page 66)

SPECIAL EQUIPMENT
instant-read thermometer

1. In a large skillet, heat the canola oil over medium heat. Add the green chiles, refried beans, epazote (if using), and a large pinch each of salt and pepper. Stir until smooth and well combined. Cook until the beans are warmed through, 3 to 4 minutes. Turn off the heat, remove the epazote (if you used it), and allow the mixture to cool slightly.

2. In a medium bowl, whisk together the sour cream, mayonnaise, lime zest, cumin, and a large pinch each of salt and pepper.

3. Spread the refried beans over the bottom of a large, flat serving platter. Layer with the sour cream mixture, guacamole, cheese, lettuce, black olives, scallions, and radishes. Sprinkle with as much or as little hot sauce as you like and serve with the homemade tortilla chips alongside.

SERVES 8 TO 12

PREP TIME
15 minutes

ACTIVE TIME
5 minutes

TOTAL TIME
25 minutes

MODERATE

The **epazote** (a pungent Mexican herb) helps with **digestion**!

If you don't feel like making **guacamole** for this dip, you can also just mash together two or three **avocados** with a pinch of salt and some lime juice and use that as your guacamole layer.

MEATBALL SLIDERS

ON HOMEMADE PRETZEL ROLLS

FOR THE PRETZEL ROLLS

1 cup warm water (105 to 115°F)

2¼ teaspoons active dry yeast (one ¼-ounce packet)

1 teaspoon sugar

1 teaspoon kosher salt

2½ cups bread flour, plus more for dusting

2 tablespoons unsalted butter, at room temperature

Vegetable oil, for greasing

¼ cup baking soda

Pretzel salt (available at Walmart or on Amazon or Nuts.com) or other coarse salt, for sprinkling

FOR THE MEATBALLS

3 tablespoons olive oil

2 garlic cloves, minced

2 medium shallots, finely chopped

Kosher salt

3 slices stale white bread, crusts removed

¾ cup buttermilk

1 large egg, beaten

1 cup finely grated Parmesan cheese (about 1 ounce)

2 tablespoons coarsely chopped fresh flat-leaf parsley

1 pound 80% lean ground beef

1 pound sweet or spicy Italian sausage, casings removed

2 cups of your favorite marinara sauce

8 slices Provolone cheese, quartered

1. Make the pretzel rolls: Pour the warm water into the bowl of a stand mixer fitted with the dough hook and sprinkle in the yeast. Set aside until the yeast starts to foam, about 5 minutes.

2. Meanwhile, in a medium bowl, whisk together the sugar, kosher salt, and bread flour. Add the flour mixture and butter to the bowl with the yeast and turn the mixer to low speed. Mix until the dough is shaggy, scraping down the sides of the bowl with a rubber spatula as needed, 1 to 2 minutes. Increase the speed to medium and mix until the dough is smooth and elastic, 6 to 7 minutes.

3. Lightly oil a large bowl. Shape the dough into a ball and place it in the bowl, turning the dough to coat with the oil. Cover with a damp kitchen towel and let rest in a warm place until doubled in size, 30 to 40 minutes.

4. Line a large baking sheet with a silicone baking mat or a large piece of parchment paper (if using parchment, heavily grease it with oil).

5. Lightly dust your work surface with flour. Transfer the dough to the floured surface and punch it down to deflate it. Knead the dough until it is smooth and no longer sticky, about 5 minutes. Divide the dough into 4 equal pieces, then cut each piece into quarters to make 16 pieces total. Roll each piece of dough into a small ball, then place it on the prepared baking sheet, seam-side down, making sure to leave enough space between the rolls to allow the dough to double in size. Cut a large "X" about ¼ inch deep into the top of each roll. Cover with a damp kitchen towel and set aside in a warm place until the rolls have nearly doubled in size, about 20 minutes.

6. Set one oven rack in the top position and another in the bottom position and preheat the oven to 425°F. Line a baking sheet with a clean kitchen towel.

RECIPE CONTINUES

PREP TIME
25 minutes

ACTIVE TIME
45 minutes

TOTAL TIME
2 hours
40 minutes
(includes rising and resting time)

MODERATE

SLIDERS

If baking your own pretzel buns feels like too much work, seek out **store-bought**. Or prep them on a quiet weekend, put them in the **freezer**, and take them out to thaw when party time rolls around.

7. Bring 8 cups water to a boil in a large, deep, straight-sided skillet and stir in the baking soda. Carefully add half the rolls to the boiling water and cook for about 30 seconds, flipping halfway through. Use a slotted spoon or spider to transfer the rolls to the towel-lined baking sheet to dry for 1 to 2 minutes. Repeat with the remaining rolls. When they've dried, transfer all the rolls back to the silicone mat– or parchment-lined baking sheet. Sprinkle the tops of the rolls generously with the pretzel salt.

8. Bake the rolls on the top rack of the oven until golden brown, 10 to 11 minutes. Move the pan to the bottom rack and bake until the rolls are deep golden brown and cooked through, 3 to 4 minutes more. Remove from the oven and let the rolls cool on the baking sheet while you prepare the meatballs.

9. Make the meatballs: Switch the oven to broil.

10. In a medium skillet, heat the olive oil over medium heat. Add the garlic, shallots, a pinch of salt, and a splash of water and cook until the shallots are soft, 5 minutes. Turn off the heat and let cool slightly.

11. Put the bread in a large bowl and pour the buttermilk over it. Set aside until the bread has soaked up most of the buttermilk, about 5 minutes. Add the egg, Parmesan, parsley, cooked shallot mixture, and 1 teaspoon salt; use your hands to stir the mixture together until combined with no large pieces of bread visible. Add the ground beef and sausage and gently combine all the ingredients with your hands until just combined (avoid overworking the mixture or the meatballs will be tough).

12. Using a ¼-cup measure to scoop the meat mixture, form it into 16 meatballs, gently patting and rolling each portion into a ball. Transfer to a large baking sheet and broil the meatballs until browned all over, 5 to 10 minutes (browning time depends greatly on the intensity of your broiler; you're just browning the meatballs—they will cook through in the sauce). Remove the meatballs from the oven and set the oven temperature to 425°F.

13. In a large saucepan, bring the tomato sauce to a low simmer over medium heat. Gently nestle the browned meatballs into the sauce, cover, and cook until the meatballs are just cooked through, about 10 minutes.

14. Cut each pretzel roll in half and place them cut-side up on a large baking sheet. Spoon a bit of sauce onto the bottom half of each roll, then top each with 1 meatball. Layer 2 pieces of provolone on each meatball. Bake until the cheese has just melted, 4 to 5 minutes. Close the sandwiches and serve immediately.

POPCORN BAR:

POPCORN WITH CURRY BUTTER,
BACON FAT POPCORN, AND
SWEET-AND-SALTY POPCORN WITH MINI MERINGUES

Bacon Fat Popcorn

Makes 12 cups ◆ *Prep time:* 5 minutes
Active time: 10 minutes ◆ *Total time:* 10 minutes ◆ *Easy*

3 tablespoons bacon fat

2/3 cup popcorn kernels

Kosher salt

Bacon bits (optional)

1. In a large heavy-bottomed stockpot or Dutch oven, melt the bacon fat over medium-high heat. When the fat starts to shimmer, add the popcorn kernels and stir to coat in the bacon fat. Cook, stirring continuously, for 1 minute, then cover the pot with a lid; you should hear the kernels start popping after 30 seconds to 1 minute. Cook, shaking the pot often to prevent the kernels from burning, until the sound of the popping kernels slows down significantly, 3 to 4 minutes. Turn off the heat but keep the lid on until the popping stops completely.

2. Remove the lid, season liberally with salt, then cover the pot again and give it a few good shakes, preferably turning it completely over with the lid on to evenly distribute the salt. Serve in a large bowl. Sprinkle with bacon bits, if desired.

◆

Who knew you could make popcorn
with **bacon fat**? I am addicted—I could
eat a **bowl every day**.

Popcorn with Curry Butter

Makes about 12 cups ◆ *Prep time:* 5 minutes
Active time: 10 minutes ◆ *Total time:* 15 minutes ◆ *Easy*

3 tablespoons unsalted butter

1 tablespoon curry powder

3 tablespoons canola oil

2/3 cup popcorn kernels

1 teaspoon kosher salt

1. In a small saucepan, combine the butter and curry powder and cook over low heat, stirring frequently, until the butter has completely melted, about 2 minutes. Turn off the heat and set aside.

2. In a large heavy-bottomed stockpot or Dutch oven, heat the canola oil over medium-high heat. When the oil starts to shimmer (this should take about 3 minutes), add the popcorn kernels and stir to coat in the oil. Cook, stirring continuously, for 1 minute, then cover the pot with a lid; you should hear the kernels start popping after 30 seconds to 1 minute. Cook, shaking the pot often to prevent the kernels from burning, until the sound of the popping kernels slows down significantly, 3 to 4 minutes. Turn off the heat but keep the lid on until the popping stops completely.

3. Remove the lid and drizzle the curry butter over the popcorn, then season with the salt. Put the lid back on (wipe it off first if it's wet with condensation) and give the pot a few good shakes so the popcorn gets evenly coated with the butter and salt. Serve in a large bowl.

RECIPE CONTINUES

Sweet-and-Salty Popcorn
with Mini Meringues

Makes about 18 cups ◆ *Prep time:* 5 minutes
Active time: 25 minutes ◆ *Total time:* 1 hour 5 minutes
Moderate

These mini meringues come courtesy of
Harper, and Neil had the idea to throw them into
salted buttered popcorn. Genius!

FOR THE MINI MERINGUES

2 large egg whites, at room temperature

Cream of tartar

Fine salt

⅓ cup sugar

FOR THE POPCORN

3 tablespoons canola oil

⅔ cup popcorn kernels

3 tablespoons unsalted butter, melted

Kosher salt

1. Make the mini meringues: Arrange two racks in the
center of the oven and preheat the oven to 200°F. Line two
baking sheets with parchment paper.

2. In a medium bowl, using a whisk or handheld mixer, beat
the egg whites and a pinch each of cream of tartar and salt
until the egg whites are foamy, about 1 minute. Increase the
speed to high (or really get your arm going) and gradually
add the sugar while beating until the egg whites form stiff,
glossy peaks, about 5 minutes more.

3. Transfer the meringue to a small piping bag fitted with a
¼-inch star tip. Pipe ¾-inch mounds of meringue (about
the size of a popped piece of popcorn) onto the prepared
baking sheets (you should get 125 to 150 meringues total).
Bake until they are completely dry and crisp, 35 to
40 minutes, rotating the baking sheets front to back and
top to bottom halfway through the cooking time. Remove
from the oven and set the baking sheets on a wire rack.
Let the meringues cool completely. (The meringues can
be cooled and stored in an airtight container at room
temperature for 2 to 3 days.)

4. Make the popcorn: In a large heavy-bottomed pot or
Dutch oven, heat the canola oil over medium-high heat.
When the oil shimmers, add the popcorn kernels and give
them a good shake. Cook, stirring continuously, for 1 minute,
then cover the pot with a lid; you should hear the kernels
start popping after 30 seconds to 1 minute. Cook, shaking
the pot often to prevent the kernels from burning, until the
sound of the popping kernels slows down significantly, 3 to
4 minutes. Turn off the heat but keep the lid on until the
popping stops completely.

5. Remove the lid, drizzle in the butter, and season liberally
with salt. Put the lid back on and give the pot a few good
shakes so that the popcorn gets evenly coated with the
butter and salt.

6. Transfer the warm popcorn to a large bowl and gently toss
with the cooled mini meringues. Serve within a few hours so
the popcorn doesn't get stale.

CHICKEN TOT PIE

One of Gideon's favorite meals is chicken potpie, and my dad once gave me a cookbook of Tater Tot recipes. Put the two together, and you get this deliciousness: a chicken potpie with Tater Tots on top! Gideon even came up with the great name.

3 bone-in, skin-on chicken breasts (about 2 pounds)

4 cups low-sodium chicken stock

1 cup water

1 pound frozen Tater Tots (about 4 cups)

4 tablespoons (½ stick) unsalted butter

2 large shallots, finely diced

Kosher salt and freshly ground black pepper

2 medium carrots, diced

2 celery stalks, diced

1 teaspoon fresh thyme leaves

¼ cup all-purpose flour

1 cup half-and-half

½ cup frozen petite peas

Hot sauce

1. Preheat the oven to 425°F.

2. In a large saucepan, combine the chicken breasts, stock, and water (the liquid should just cover the chicken) and bring the liquid to a simmer over medium-high heat. Reduce the heat to medium-low and gently simmer, uncovered, until the chicken is just cooked through, flipping the chicken once and skimming off any foam from the surface as it cooks, about 20 minutes. Transfer to a large bowl and set aside to cool slightly (leave the liquid in the saucepan). Once cooled, shred using two forks (discard the skin and bones) and set aside.

3. Return the liquid in the saucepan to medium-high heat and bring to a boil. Boil until it has reduced to 2 cups, skimming off any foam that rises to the surface, about 20 minutes.

4. While the chicken cooks, bake the Tater Tots on a baking sheet until crisp, about 15 minutes; set aside. Keep the oven on.

5. In a large skillet, melt the butter over medium heat. Add the shallots and a pinch of salt and cook, stirring occasionally, until tender, 4 to 5 minutes. Add the carrots, celery, and a pinch of salt and cook, stirring occasionally, until the carrots are tender, 9 to 10 minutes. Stir in the thyme and flour and cook, stirring continuously, for 1 minute more. Stir in the reduced stock and half-and-half, increase the heat to high to bring the liquid to a boil, then reduce the heat to low and simmer, stirring frequently, until thickened, 4 to 5 minutes. Turn off the heat and stir in the shredded chicken and the peas. Season the mixture with salt, pepper, and hot sauce to taste.

6. Transfer the Tater Tots to a large bowl and wipe off the baking sheet. Place a 2-quart baking dish on the baking sheet and fill it with the chicken mixture. Arrange the Tater Tots in an even layer over the top, then bake until the filling is bubbling and the Tater Tots are very crispy, 20 to 25 minutes. Let stand for 5 minutes before serving.

PREP TIME
15 minutes

ACTIVE TIME
25 minutes

TOTAL TIME
2 hours 10 minutes

MODERATE

This pie can be **dressed up** in many different ways. Want to put an Asian spin on it? Add **sriracha** instead of regular hot sauce and replace the peas with frozen shelled edamame. Maybe a little **Tex-Mex flair**? Add a couple of spoonfuls of chopped Hatch chiles to up the heat factor. If you are making it for kids, serve the hot sauce on the side.

LEFTOVER CANDY BROWNIES

1¼ cups (2½ sticks) unsalted butter, cut into ½-inch pieces, plus more for greasing

1⅓ cups bittersweet chocolate chips (8 ounces)

1⅓ cups milk chocolate chips (8 ounces)

¾ cup all-purpose flour

2 teaspoons baking powder

¾ teaspoon fine salt

1⅓ cups sugar

2 teaspoons vanilla extract

4 large eggs

As much leftover chocolate holiday candy as your heart desires (or at least enough to cover the top of the brownies)

1. Preheat the oven to 350°F. Lightly grease a 9 by 13-inch cake pan, then line it with two pieces of parchment paper perpendicular to each other and overhanging all sides of the pan. Lightly grease the parchment.

2. In a large microwave-safe bowl, combine the butter and both chocolates and microwave in 15-second intervals, stirring after each, until the chips are just melted and the mixture is combined, 1 to 2 minutes. Set the chocolate aside to cool slightly, 10 to 15 minutes. (You want the mixture to still be slightly warm, but not hot.)

3. In a medium bowl, whisk together the flour, baking powder, and salt and set aside. Stir the sugar and vanilla into the still-warm chocolate mixture and whisk until combined. Whisk in the eggs until the mixture is smooth and well combined. Whisk the flour mixture into the chocolate mixture until just incorporated. Pour the batter into the prepared pan. Lightly press the leftover chocolate candies into the top of the batter (assorted chocolate truffles, such as Ferrero Rocher, are particularly delicious here!).

4. Bake until the top of the batter just starts to puff up and feels dry to the touch, about 25 minutes (it won't be fully baked yet). Remove from the oven, gently drop the pan onto the counter to release air, and return the brownies to the oven. Bake until a cake tester or toothpick inserted into the outer edge of the brownies comes out clean, 10 to 15 minutes more. The center will seem underdone, but these are particularly fudgy brownies, so it is very important not to overbake. Remove from the oven and set the pan on a wire rack. Let the brownie block cool completely, at least 4 hours. Use the parchment paper handles to gently lift the brownie block out of the cake pan and cut it into 24 pieces. The brownies can be served immediately or stored in an airtight container at room temperature for up to 5 days.

MAKES 24 BROWNIES

PREP TIME
10 minutes

ACTIVE TIME
15 minutes

TOTAL TIME
5 hours 10 minutes
(includes cooling time)

EASY

This is the **perfect way** to get rid of any **lingering** holiday candy— just throw it in the batter and bake it! When you are done with a pan of these, you are ready to go and do the fresh start brunch (page 252)!

ACKNOWLEDGMENTS

Amy Neunsinger, thank you for being such a joy to be around, and for the stunning food beauties—you made Mozart outta my sliders!

Danielle Levitt, thank you for bringing the party. Every time.

Thank you, **Adeena Sussman**, for your knowledge and your ability to keep me on track and away from tangents.

Laura Nolan, thank you for being a fantastic boss and for captaining our ship along its delicious course.

Frances Boswell, please thank your brain for all of your crazy and marvelous ideas.

Pam Morris, thank you for your eye and gorgeous aesthetic.

Andrew Mitchell, **Vanessa Vazquez**, **Denise Ginley**, and **Imogen Kwok**—thank you for always being there on set ready to jump in wherever needed. You guys rock!

Lauren Accardo, thank you for your lack of social life and for the long hours you put in to help make this book happen. Additionally, thank you for being way smarter than me without rubbing it in my face.

To Morgan Hedden at Grand Central Publishing: Thank you for championing me and pushing this project. Without you none of this would have been made.

Tareth Mitch: I do not know how you survived reading this book over and over. Your eye and persistence are incredible.

Laura Palese: Your creativity in designing this book is magical. Every color, font, and space you have picked is just right. Thank you for making me look so good.

Chelsea Hayes: You are a doll and I have loved working with you every step of the way. Thanks for getting my mug out for the world to see.

Michael Serrato: Even though you are not physically in the book, so much of you is. Thank you for the support and every piece of pushy advice I didn't ask for. I love you more than you know.

Lee Schrager: For being such a stand-up friend and helping me launch this book with flair.

Mark Pastore: Your generosity is beyond. I cannot thank you enough for your gifts and your friendship.

Neil, thanks for putting up with my antics A and for showing me only love and support in the face of great adversity. I value your opinion more than anyone's. You are my rock; thanks for being so strong.

Harper and **Gideon**, thank you for tasting all of the failed recipe tests, for your input no matter how brutal, and above all for being such a big part of why I love cooking. Thank you for giving me the time I needed to make this happen.

Most of all, thank **you** for buying and using this cookbook! I hope you enjoy these recipes as much as I, my family, and my friends have. May all of your parties be a smash, and may all of your guests leave delightfully stuffed. Happy cooking!

The following people graciously appeared in the photos that bring my parties to life. Thank you for your time, enthusiasm, and fabulous energy that fill the photos with so much joy and beauty.

SPRING
Kerry Butler; Segi and Sumaya Mazzarino; Avery, Grey, and Nicole Kelly; Gemma Rathore; August Gold; Caroline Shaw; Dan Burtka; Stacey Griffith; Leo and Kris Lythgoe; Mason Lee; Jackson Meadowcroft; Sydney Callahan; Cobie Smulders; Becky Baeling; Melba Wilson; Claire Rothrock; Paul Graves; Sherif Sherikama; Lizzie Tisch; Allison Connor; Ravi Singh

SUMMER
Georgina Treen; Ludivine and Rima Levitt; Ever Smith; August, Athena, and Magnus Speyer; Kobi Garrett; Miles, Mia, and Nicole Middleton; Danielle Levitt; Adrian Salpeter; Sarah Zajas; Jonathan Bayme; Christiana Chin; Anne-Cecile Speyer

FALL
Noa Awaku-Tatum; Tai and Emi Stolzberg; Kendrick Opoku-Ansah; Lily Gallagher; Charles Wallece; Lady Bunny; Kate Jennings Grant; Linda Dahl; Becca Doyle; Damian Accosta; Lauren Accardo

WINTER
Oliver, Henry, and Georgina Treen; Kate and Luke Reinders; Marti Gould Cummings; James Gunter; Greg Lawrence; Jeffery Povero; Paul McGill; Maisie Wilhelm; Sierra Boggess; Montego Glover; Derrick Baskin; Daniel J. Watts; Jonathan Lind

Thanks as well to KitchenAid; Cuisinart; Le Creuset; Pat LaFrieda; Sid Wainer; King Arthur Flour; Kim Seybert; Lisa Friedman; Crow Canyon Home; Williams Sonoma; Crate & Barrel; ROE Caviar; Veuve Clicquot; Pottery Barn Teen; Bloomingdale's; QSquared; Kate Spade; Meri Meri

INDEX

ABOUT THE AUTHOR

DAVID BURTKA is an award-winning and sought-after host, chef, caterer, and actor. He has appeared and cooked on *The Barefoot Contessa, Home Made Simple, Every Day with Rachael Ray, Wendy Williams, The Kitchen*, and others. He has been a guest judge on *Beat Bobby Flay, RuPaul's Drag Race, Worst Cooks in America, Top Chef Masters*, and *Iron Chef America*. David's recipes have been featured in *Food & Wine*, the *Food Network Magazine, People, Us Weekly* and on Kitchn.com.

David studied culinary arts at Le Cordon Bleu and trained under Gina DePalma at the acclaimed New York City restaurant Babbo, with Thomas Keller at Bouchon, and with Iron Chef Cat Cora. David then created the Hollywood-based catering company, Gourmet M.D., where he threw elaborate parties and prepared meals for Hollywood elite (both actual and self-proclaimed). David's Food Network special, *Life's a Party with David Burtka*, aired in 2016 and was awarded a Telly Award and first prize at the New York Film and TV Awards.

Prior to his career in food, David was seen on Broadway starring in *It Shoulda Been You, The Goat or Who Is Sylvia*, and *Gypsy*, for which he won a Fred Astaire Award. He also earned the Clarence Derwent Award for his role in Edward Albee's *The Play About the Baby*. Burtka's film credits include *Dance-Off, Annie and the Gypsy, A Very Harold & Kumar 3-D Christmas*, and Woody Allen's *Hollywood Ending*. He also had a recurring role on *How I Met Your Mother* and other television series such as *The West Wing, On the Lot*, and *American Horror Story–Freak Show*.

David grew up outside of Detroit, Michigan, and earned a BFA from the University of Michigan before studying at the William Esper Studios in New York. Today, David lives in Harlem, New York, with his husband, Neil Patrick Harris, and their twin children, Gideon and Harper.